Sociology and Jurisprudence of Leon Petrażycki

RUSSIAN AND EAST EUROPEAN CENTER

Published in conjunction with the

OFFICE OF INTERNATIONAL
PROGRAMS AND STUDIES

SOCIOLOGY AND JURISPRUDENCE OF LEON PETRAŻYCKI

JAN GORECKI, Editor

UNIVERSITY OF ILLINOIS PRESS
Urbana Chicago London

Manufactured in the United States of America

Library of Congress Cataloging in Publication Data

Górecki, Jan.
Sociology and jurisprudence of Leon Petrazycki.

Bibliography: p.
Includes index.
1. Petrazhit͡skiĭ, Lev Iosifovich, 1867-1931.
2. Jurisprudence—Addresses, essays, lectures.
3. Sociological jurisprudence—Addresses, essays, lectures. 4. Sociology—Addresses, essays, lectures.
I. Title.
Law 301.1'15 75-38551
ISBN 0-252-00525-2

To the Center for Advanced Study in the Behavioral Sciences
—my first home in America

J.G.

Contents

Leon Petrażycki.

Preface

Leon Petrażycki (1867-1931) was a professor at St. Petersburg University and at the University of Warsaw.[1] He was one of those few humanists who succeeded in building an original and consistent theoretical system; it encompassed philosophy of science, sociological theory, sociology of law, social policy, psychology, and theory of law and of morals. The system was prompted by his social ideal: the state of active and universal benevolence of men. He believed in the adjustive evolution of mankind toward the ideal, and he considered law and morality as two motivating forces of the evolution.

To approach the ideal efficiently, a peculiar kind of social policy—social engineering through law—has to be applied; that is, a conscious use of law to educate and socialize men. To be able to use law as a tool of engineering, one has to learn what the peculiar characteristics of the tool are; however, lawyers had never been able to reach agreement on these characteristics. That was why Petrazycki moved toward developing a new legal theory. In order to do that he built an original methodology—a new logic of scientific theorizing. Then, applying his methodological proposals, he found legal (as well as moral) phenomena not in norms but in the human mind. To develop a psychological theory of law (and morality), he reshaped the psychology of his day. Anticipating further developments of the behavioral science, he articulated many ideas of classical conditioning and instrumental learning theories in a manner that has never since been excelled. On the basis of his theory of human behavior, he presented law and morality as peculiar kinds of

[1]The Polish transliteration of his name is used in this book (from now on, however, omitting the dot over the *z*), and it should be pronounced "Petrazhitski." Leo v. Petrazycki appears on his works published in German, Lev I. Petrazhitskii—on those in Russian.

powerful drives. This approach appeared fruitful: it enabled him to illuminate and reshape the whole field of general sociology, sociology of law, and legal philosophy. He designed a new theory of social evolution: it was Darwinist, but avoided all the failures of Social Darwinism; and it claimed discovery of trends, not laws of social development, thus avoiding the historicist failure. An original theory of state and economy has been offered, referring to the organizational and distributive functions of legal drives, as well as a theory of justice, a functional theory of rights and duties, new criticism of the "natural law" doctrine, a theory of intuitive *vs.* positive law, a sociopsychological theory of revolutions, and a new perspective of legal subcultures. All this makes a comprehensive system of rare greatness, locating its author in the first row of grand theorists of man in society—on a par with Spencer and Durkheim, Marx and Weber.

Petrazycki's main works appeared in Russian, and a selection of his writings was published in English in 1955.[2] What the present volume intends to provide is a concise and critical presentation of his views in the context of more recent developments in scientific knowledge. That is why the contributions to follow were written from the standpoint of the structural-functional theory of society, symbolic interactionism, legal realism, post-realistic jurisprudence, and so on. This should bring Petrazycki into the current frame of reference, promote critical appraisal of both Petrazycki and more recent thinkers, and help in absorbing and utilizing all those elements of his system which surpass what has been later proposed by others.

Thanks are due to several persons and institutions who helped in the preparation of this book. First, to the Office of International Programs and Studies, and to the Russian and East European Center, both at the University of Illinois, for financial support; and, in particular, to Ralph T. Fisher, Jr., Director of the Russian and East European Center.

Wiesław Lang (University of Toruń Law Faculty) and Peter Maggs (University of Illinois Law College) gave their thought and time to discuss the manuscript at a meeting of the contributors held in September, 1973, at Urbana. Kathleen Seeds typed the manuscript with dedication. The editors of the *Journal of Philosophy* and *Przeglad Socjologiczny* kindly agreed to the reproduction of the articles by Maria Ossowska and Jerzy Lande.

---

[2]*Law and Morality: Leon Petrazycki* (Cambridge, Mass.: Harvard University Press, 1955).

Laura Appelbaum, the editorial assistant, was most helpful in editing, proofreading, and preparing the index and the bibliography. She also made important critical comments on the contents of various chapters. Indeed, her contributions were invaluable.

My warmest thanks go, as always, to Danuta.

Jan Gorecki

CHAPTER

1

Leon Petrazycki

JAN GORECKI

"No small part of the law's function is to make men good," as a well-known dictum of Mr. Justice Brandeis goes. This had become, half a century earlier, the leading notion of Leon Petrazycki's legal and social philosophy. He opposed his contemporaries, who thought of law as an implement to balance and protect interests—a view influential until now. He considered law an educative tool to socialize men in the spirit of mutual benevolence (or, to use his original expression, of universal, active, rational love). To utilize law as a tool, a science of legal policy—of social engineering through law—had to be developed. Its development soon became Petrazycki's most cherished idea, and it remained so. To implement it, he architectured a broad and consistent theoretical system encompassing, in particular, general methodology, psychology, sociology, and legal and moral theory. The system is remarkable irrespective of its practical implications. Nevertheless, it has been designed as a theoretical basis for social action: Petrazycki's was the scholarship of involvement and social concern. The time and place of his activity may, at least partially, account for this. (It may also account for the fact that he is barely known in the English-speaking countries.)

Born in 1867, to a Polish gentry family, he graduated in 1890 from the Kiev Law School and spent the following two years on a scholarship in Berlin, where he published two major works in German. One of them, *Die Lehre vom Einkommen*—a famous criticism of the then discussed drafts of the German Civil Code—contained, in the appendix, the germ of his future system; the revised version of the appendix was published in Russia in 1896-97 as the *Introduction to the Science of Legal Policy.* Appointed, in 1898, Professor of Philosophy of Law at the St. Petersburg University Law School (where he also served as the first elected dean when the university was granted autonomy), he published all his major works within the following fifteen years; among them, *On the Motives of Human Behavior, Introduction to the Study of Law and Morality, Theory of Law and State.* He also became involved in politics: a constitutional democrat and active liberal, in 1906 he was elected to the first Russian legislature, which was dissolved months later. Having signed the Viborg manifest—a protest against the dissolution—he was convicted and briefly incarcerated. After the revolution of February, 1917—in the brief period of parliamentary democracy in Russia—he was appointed justice of the Supreme Court. When the Soviets won, he left for Warsaw where the chair of sociology was established for him by the School of Law. There he wrote and taught until his self-imposed death in 1931. Thus his studies, and the most fruitful years of his scholarly activity, coincided with a particularly troubled period of change and upheaval in Russia: of unruly industrial growth, famines in the countryside, reactionary measures of Alexandr III and Nicolai II, defeat in the war with Japan, violence and revolution of 1905, liberal measures in 1906, and the following ruthless regime which increased strife and radical tendencies. Petrazycki's social concern was apparently stimulated by the social problems he came across.[1]

How could law be used to socialize men? To answer, one has first to discover how law, in general, influences human behavior. This implies relying on a viable theory of law. However, in Petrazycki's opinion, no such theory has ever been offered. What, then, ought to be done to develop it? Or more broadly, how, in general, should theories be made? Only sound methodology can provide an answer, and, consequently, Petrazycki started building his system by pondering on ways of scientific theorizing.[2]

He considered selecting a proper subject matter for a theory—that is, things or events to become its designates—as the first necessary step. To be proper, the designates must fulfill three requirements. First, they must have some characteristic(s) peculiar to all of them, and to them only. Second, since universal statements of scientific theory can be pronounced only about an unlimited number of things or events, they must not be restricted to a closed set of individual items (a group of designates which meets the two requirements is called "class" by Petrazycki). Third, they must be suitable for fertile theorizing, that is, for a theory with great descriptive and explanatory power. The thus selected class of designates should be given a name. This will often be an ordinary language term. Its proposed meaning will sometimes match its meaning in the ordinary language; for example, the meaning of "plant" as a name for designates of botany, or "bird," of ornithology. More frequently, especially in the field of human behavior, the proposed meaning of the name will depart from its ordinary meaning: it will denote an arbitrarily selected class. (Thus, giving a name implies an inverse process of arbitrary definition of the name: there is no prior asking what does the name mean, but how the selected designates of a theory are to be named.) Only if the designates are selected and named in this manner can the most basic requirement of adequacy of theories be met. The requirement claims that theories be made of statements which hold with respect to all, and only to the class of selected designates.

Where can designates for an adequate theory of law be found? Traditionally, legal theory treats state-made (or legally sanctioned) norms as its subject. However, Petrazycki considers state-made (or legally sanctioned) law as only a portion of a broader class of legal phenomena—a portion having exactly the same characteristics as the broader class. Thus, limiting designates of "law" to this portion—an approach resulting from habits of the legal profession—rules out an adequate legal theory. Consequently, it results in bad theorizing.[3] Defining law as state-made norms implies tautology, since the state itself is a legal fact. Limiting it to legally sanctioned norms is inapplicable to norms of international law, and also implies tautology, or infinite regress: a norm A is legal if it is accompanied by norm B which sanctions violation of A; but B, to be legal, must be accompanied by a norm sanctioning violation of B; and so forth. Furthermore, theorizing on norms, if possible at all, is less fertile than theorizing on real things or events (like physical bodies or processes that the bodies go through). Consequently, Petrazycki opts for realistic, not normative, jurisprudence. Of course, one can look for real things or events to be called "law" either in relations among men (for example, between debtors and creditors) or in human minds. Petrazycki considers the former alternative as reification of law, and he thus accepts the latter: law can be found within ourselves, as a peculiar kind of experience. Consequently, he turns to psychology to discover and analyze the legal experiences.[4]

Psychology of his day divided all mental processes into three categories. One of them, the will, was considered active—a tendency toward something. The two others, cognition (sensory perceptions and images) and emotions (pleasure and pain), were considered as passive. Petrazycki challenged the taxonomy: he claimed discovery of the fourth element stimulating (alone, or in conjunction with the other elements) all human and animal behavior. The discovery was due to introspection: observation of one's own mental processes, and body movements resulting from them; and inferring contents of the mental processes of others, by analogy, from their body movements.

He named the new element "impulsion." Hunger, thirst, the sexual drive, fear, curiosity, and hunting drives are a few instances. Impulsions are not just passive or active, but bilateral: the subject experiences (passively) something stimulating, and responds with an (active) urge. The urge may be attractive, like hunger or sex, or aversive, like fear or disgust.

The urge affects behavior: it results in psychological and physiological changes, and in various body movements which differ from one to another kind of impulsion. For instance, hunger brings about the appearance of images and thoughts of food, and, if acute, it represses other mental processes—other impulsions, intellect, will. Appropriate glands, nerves, and muscles undergo stimulation at the sight or the idea of food which results, in men and animals, in salivation, movements of the tongue, lips, cheeks, and so on. Food repulsion results in very different conduct: the sight, smell, or taste of decayed meat results in glandular, nervous, and muscular processes which either prevent the food from getting into the mouth and stomach or cause its removal from there. Behavior brought about by many other kinds of impulsions—the sexual or hunting drive, thirst, fear, curiosity—also displays specific characteristics. Each of them functions as an important implement in the process of adjustment: they turn the human or infrahuman organism into an instrument able to perform a specific biological function—eating, drinking, rejecting harmful substances, procurement of food, reproduction, and so forth. All other elements of mental life play a supplementary role only. In particular the passive elements, like pleasure or pain, influence behavior only if they arouse impulsions, and not by themselves.

Each of the thus far presented impulsions is followed by a peculiar kind of behavior; that is why Petrazycki calls them "specific," or "special." He contrasts them with another category—the "blanket" impulsions—which may result in any kind of behavior: they stimulate toward or against the conduct whose idea is being simultaneously experienced. There are here impulsions aroused by commands: orders, in particular sudden and forceful ones, tend to bring about urges toward conduct which corresponds with the contents of the order. Also included here are aesthetic impulsions, which encourage any conduct perceived as beautiful, glamorous, or elegant—like acts of courage or noiseless eating; or against any conduct perceived as ugly, hideous, or vulgar—like fleeing the battlefield or undressing at a formal dinner.[5]

Every day we experience a great number of impulsions which direct our behavior, but the majority of them are too weak to even be perceived: they are unconscious. Their weakness is useful: strong urges consume large amounts of energy, sometimes up to exhaustion, and waste can be avoided only if the force of impulsions does not exceed the amount necessary to perform their biological or social function. Thus, being as faint as possible, they should intensify if performing the function meets difficulties; and indeed, they do. That is why by counteracting them we are able to strengthen them, bring them into full consciousness, and observe their action. For instance, hunger, thirst, the urge for physical activity, for work, or for the company of others increase if counteracted, and repulsions against eating harmful substances, being burnt, or touching an open eye increase at attempts to break the prohibitions. Provocation is another way of making them strong. The sight and smell of appetizing food increases hunger, petting increases the sexual drive, and the ill-conceived steps of those in power increase political impulsions of insulted groups. Both counteracting and provoking may also be applied as "mental experiments": appetitive impulsions may increase at imagining thirst or hunger, repulsive impulsions, at imagining eating anything abominable or standing on the edge of a precipice.

There is one class of blanket impulsions which are of particular importance for these considerations: the impulsions of duty. They emerge in response to ideas of (present, future, or just imaginary) conduct which is being evaluated as intrinsically right or wrong. The idea of oneself or someone else committing an act of perjury, cheating, or murder causes repulsion: an experience of (my own or someone else's) duty not to do it. The idea of fulfilling a promise or saving a drowning child arouses the feeling of duty toward positive action. Petrazycki calls this class "ethical impulsions." They also are predominantly weak and often unconscious. However, counteracting and provoking makes them perceivable, and frequently powerful (for example, their strengthening results from persuading one's friend that he should not steal or cheat while he disagrees and argues; vivid ideas of wrongdoing coming from the press or novels have a similar provoking influence).

Having identified ethical impulsions, Petrazycki claims discovery of the legal phenomenon in the human mind. The ethical impulsions are of two kinds. Some of them are being experienced as duty to which another person's right corresponds; for example, promisor's duty as matched with promisee's right. The others are being experienced as duties to which no rights correspond; for example, the evangelic duty of turning the other cheek or of almsgiving does not imply corresponding claims on the part of the assaulter or the beggar. The ethical impulsions of the latter kind have been called "morality" by Petrazycki. The former have been called "law," and considered as the proper subject of an adequate legal theory.[6]

This is an unusual approach. First, a new, mutually exclusive demarcation line between law and morality is being drawn: customarily, the officially implemented norms have been considered as legal, and those internalized as moral, which made law and morality intersecting fields. Second, and more important, the shift from legal norms to legal feelings (of which norms are just expressions), and the rejection of norms as a conceivable subject of legal theory, means an arbitrary break with traditional jurisprudence. This, of course, broadens the field of law, which would now include not only duty-right experiences corresponding with official codes, but also the experiences of children (like claims for promised candy), gangsters (claims for loot sharing), and madmen. Morality, too, would encompass all feelings of duty (if not accompanied by feelings of right): those experienced by the broader population, saints, tyrants, children, gangsters, madmen, and so on. This clearly implies a meta-ethical theory, focusing on structural and functional characteristics of legal and moral facts, without admitting, a priori, any particular legal or moral devices; that is, without limiting the analysis to one or another set of specific norms. Thus, it pertains to all possible laws and moralities: official and not, experienced by many or few, good and evil. In this meaning, Petrazycki's is a value-free theory of law and morals.

The thus identified legal and moral impulsions are among the main stimuli of the social actions of men. The moral ones are somewhat of a luxury: they stimulate exceptional rather than broadly expected behavior. (However, in the course of social development many of them become legal: what had been perceived as a gracious obligation by the few noble-minded becomes a widespread experience encompassing rightful claims on the part of the beneficiaries; for example, the duty of equal treatment of minorities in many nations.)[7] Consequently, their social role is narrower than that of the legal impulsions. Moreover, the legal impulsions are stronger: containing not only the feeling of duty, but also of right, they tend to bring about a greater pressure on those legally bound; and they stimulate those who experience their own rights —a stimulation indispensable to the creation of a free citizen and to the development of various kinds of social activities, in particular the economic.

The last characteristic of legal impulsions—the stimulating force of claims—implies dangers: if mutual rights and duties of individuals or groups are not clearly and uniformly defined, conflicting claims easily result in aggression and destruction of contesting persons and groups, sometimes of whole societies. On the other hand, their precision and uniformity coordinates impulsions, and, consequently, the mutual behavior of those duty bound and claimants; hence the need for uniformity of views on mutual rights and obligations. This need is being met by the development of uniform sets of norms. The sets are produced, on the societal level, by legal customs, legislative enactments, precedents; on a smaller group level by parents, school boards, gang leaders, and so on. To bring about the uniformity of views, the norms must be clear and mutually consistent. However, for various reasons, especially the ambiguity of the terms which they use, lawmakers are neither able to reach a suitable degree of precision nor to coordinate norms into fully consistent systems. Consequently, to enhance uniformity, interpretation of norms has been performed by the class of legal scholars—from the Pharisees to Roman jurists to modern advocates of conceptual jurisprudence.[8] (A similar function—on which Petrazycki does not elaborate—is being performed by the judiciary, in particular by the supreme courts which, in various nations, play the role of living dictionaries by defining ambiguous legal terms.)

Petrazycki's legal and moral theory consists of two parts. One part deals with the analysis of legal and moral facts, the other with their functioning. The first converges partially with the traditional field of analytical jurisprudence. However, the field is being looked at from a new perspective, in particular due to the distinction between intuitive and positive law (and morality).[9]

Positive law means a legal impulsion encompassing the image of some prior law making fact as its source, like the enactment of a statute or a court decision; whereas intuitive law means an autonomous impulsion, experienced as binding by itself, without coincident thinking of any law-making fact. The law-making facts (called "normative facts" by Petrazycki) may include not only statutory enactments or court judgments, but also established legal habits, pronouncements of gods, prophets, chieftains, parents, slaveowners, gang bosses, and so forth. Thus, if a husband experiences his duty and his wife's right to fidelity without even thinking about family code, religious command, or any other source establishing the obligation, his legal impulsion is intuitive; while the impulsion of a driver who, having road regulations in mind, overcomes the temptation to exceed the speed limit, is positive[10] (of course, the instance assumes that he is motivated by a feeling of duty, and not by fear of sanction). Official positive law is here one important subdivision. Its impulsions have two characteristics. First, like all positive law, they encompass images of law-making facts. Second, they are officially protected: the feelings of duty and right of which they consist are being warranted and enforced by state officials. To express it simply, however, in a language rejected by Petrazycki: official positive law denotes legal experiences referring to the "legal norms in force," that is, to law as understood by the legal profession.

The distinctions are important: they reflect major differences. Referring to images of established law-making facts, positive law, in particular the official, is more uniform within the social group than the intuitive law which may differ from man to man. Changes of widespread intuitive law are flexible and continuous, and, on the whole, respond to evolving social needs (on which more will be said below); whereas changing the positive law assumes arbitrary action: the establishment of new law-making facts, like the enactment of a new statute. Consequently positive law, in particular the official, often lags behind the broadly experienced intuitive legal impulsions. This lagging is the main reason for the discrepancy between intuitive and positive law, especially official positive law, in various societies. (In other terms, and less formally, the lagging is the main reason for the discrepancy between widely experienced legal conscience and the legal norms in force.) Plurality of groups and classes is another reason: the intuitive law of each group may differ, while the official positive law is the same for the whole society. The larger the discrepancy, the stronger the general perception of the social system as unjust, and the dissatisfaction with it. This results in various pressures from intuitive law. Some of them work through judges and legal scholars who interpret the legal norms in force in a manner warranting decisions as close to their intuitive law as possible. Others bring about a broader change: the pressure of widespread intuitive law often results in new law-making facts (like the enactment of a new statute), that is, in the transformation of the positive official law. Sometimes obsolete norms fall, under the influence of the new intuitive law, into desuetude without any formal repeal. If, however, because of the egoism of powerful groups interested in preserving the existing order important discrepancies cannot be removed, the intensity of the intuitive law of the masses grows and brings about a widespread, powerful drive for change and a hatred of the existing social system, eventually resulting in revolution. Thus, an increase in the impulsive power of intuitive law explains revolutions more adequately than (traditionally referred to) class conflicts: indeed, in many societies, slaves, serfs, the poor had spent centuries under the dominance of privileged classes without ever revolting, provided that they considered the legal norms in force as just, that is, as being in accord with their intuitive law.[11]

Legal impulsions of all the above kinds perform a number of vital functions. First, they account for the emergence of power within social groups, in particular the state. What is the state (if the basic, existential meaning is ascribed to the term "is")? Petrazycki rejects various traditional, reifying theories, organic and other. He understands by "power" a peculiar kind of legal impulsion: some men experience their right to demand obedience from others, while others experience their duty to obey. Those impulsions, made uniform by uniform sets of norms, stimulate coordinated human behavior: powerholders give orders and control the behavior of others, while the others comply.

There are important differences among rights attributed to various kinds of powerholders. Some of the rights are perceived as specific (for example, those of university superiors), others as general (parental authority), some as exercised in the interests of the subordinates (parental authority), others in the interests of the powerholders (rights of slaveowners). Moreover, the rights often differ in rank: the growing complexity of social groups results in a multitude of powerholders and in the emergence of their hierarchies. All these distinctions enabled Petrazycki to define the state. He first identified one group of powerholders: those whose rights are experienced not only as general, and exercised in the interests of subordinates, but also as supreme, that is, not subject to any higher-ups. If their power links the social group, the group is "independent." The independent groups are of two kinds. Some of them at lower levels of social development are tribal, that is, limited, at least in principle, to kinsmen. Others are not limited in this way: they are called "states" by Petrazycki. Thus, state means an independent nontribal social group; it is linked by impulsions of supreme power, and by coordinated behavior stimulated by these impulsions.[12] (Of course, other experiences may additionally, and strongly, cement the group; for example, solidarity, patriotism, and so on.)

Distribution of goods is another important function of legal experiences. Property, individual or collective, consists in legal impulsions:

owners experience their right to possess, use, dispose, and all others experience the duty not to interfere. Rights established by contracts, quasi-contracts, and torts imply experiencing the right to demand and the duty to fulfill on the part of creditors and debtors, respectively. Here again, the impulsions become uniform due to uniform sets of norms; and the uniformity results in a coordinated system of economic behavior.[13]

Thus, the legal impulsions produce a coordinated system of social behavior, in particular political and economic—"a permanent and strictly defined order, binding for all . . . and justifying expectations of those who undertake economic or other activities";[14] (which explains the "strong association of the terms 'law' and 'order' in the minds of lawyers and laymen").[15] To this Petrazycki adds another function: he considers legal experiences as the most important factor of social change.

Social change comprises the subject of Petrazycki's sociology. His sociology is evolutionary.[16] Mankind develops, however inconsistently, from lower to higher levels of social adjustment: men become better socialized, with the state of universal benevolence as the final destination. There are various forces which account for the development; among them morality, aesthetics, education—especially provided by the universities.[17] Law is one of the forces, and, due to its characteristics (as presented above), it is more powerful than the others. From the early stages of social development, aversive impulsions of intuitive law emerge and spread as a psychological response to behavior harmful for the group, and attractive impulsions emerge and spread as responses to useful behavior. (This happens in a process which is reminiscent of natural selection: the adaptive experiences tend to survive, and the dysfunctional to disappear.) Then, due to the need for uniformity, the intuitive impulsions produce law-making facts, uniform sets of norms, and impulsions of positive law. Under the impact of these experiences, both intuitive and positive, members of the group become better socialized. Therefore, legal impulsions of somewhat changed contents—proper for a better socialized group—are needed. They subsequently emerge and spread in the process of the (unconscious) adjustment of intuitive legal impulsions to the new level of development of the group. Again, due to the influence of the intuitive law on the positive, they bring about new law-making facts and new sets of norms, and resultant positive impulsions. This implies a long series of changes in law and in human character under mutual impact (other factors, especially moral and aesthetic experiences, play a similar but less powerful role here). Petrazycki's analysis of legal history claims to discover some regularities in this process. First, the better socialized a given group, the more the law demands from everyone with respect to his fellow men. Second, legal incentives change from primitive to more advanced, for example, from compulsion and fear as stimuli inducing men to work, to economic motivation produced by the law of contracts, that is, by the forces of the market. Third, very strong motivational pressure of law, for example, cruel punitive measures which are necessary with respect to unsocialized man decrease in the course of development. The process, whatever its inconsistencies and setbacks, does in the long run educate men toward better socialization, solidarity, benevolence.

The process goes on, as hinted above, unconsciously: intuitive legal experiences change without the knowledge, on the part of those who experience them, of the adjustive character of the changes within the broader, evolutionary trend. However, the process can be consciously directed. The mutual relationship of intuitive and positive law is not limited to the influence of the former on the latter: there is also an opposite impact. In particular, the officially implemented law-making facts and the resultant norms in force produce new positive legal impulsions. Subsequently, the impulsions get transformed into the intuitive: obligations and rights, originally perceived as an outcome of the legal codes, become experienced as binding and just in themselves. Thus, lawmakers can purposefully shape the (positive and intuitive) legal mind of man, influence the ethos of the social group, and, consequently, smooth and speed up the otherwise unconsciously emerging ethical progress. This is exactly the role of social engineering through law as understood and recommended by Pertrazycki[18]—the legal policy to be developed on the ground of his psychological jurisprudence and evolutionary sociology.

The thus outlined system is remarkably original. This is particularly true with respect to its juridical part: making the legal experiences the subject matter of a consistent theory of law and state was an unprecedented step in the history of jurisprudence. This is also true of its other components, in particular sociology and psychology. The sociology explicitly refers to Darwinism. However, it makes an original continuation of and response to Darwin's philosophy, sharply contrasting with various Social Darwinist notions. Social Darwinists applied the theory of natural selection (and of adaptive modifications of the living species) to human society. Some of them, most notably Spencer, extended the theory to the whole universe, human society included, while others, like Gumplowicz or Sumner, made a social analog to it. They considered the struggle for "survival of the fittest" as the necessary outcome of the struggle among individuals and among social groups. From the natural law of the survival of the fittest ethical conclusions were derived: belief in the moral value of social inequality, of laissez faire economy and the ensuing defeat of the weak—a familiar confusion of nature and morality identifying the "natural" with the good.

Petrazycki also considers the struggle for survival as the main determinant of social change. This is, however, a "struggle for survival" among impulsions, in particular among ethical impulsions: emerging in the process of social adjustment they compete among themselves, and those of them that favor the good of the group become more common while those which are detrimental tend to die off. The "natural selection" of ethical experiences provides the basic mechanism for social change—for progress toward better socialization of man. This moralistic evolutionism refers to Darwin; however, it clearly differs from all the Social Darwinist doctrines. Moreover, it claims discovery of tendencies only, not laws of social development, thus avoiding the historicist failure, characteristic of many evolutionary philosophies.

Petrazycki's psychology, providing a partial explanation for his theory of social evolution, breaks with traditional, atomistic treatment of mental life. Impulsions become its most important, integrative component. Analysis of various drives denoted by the term excels, in many respects, later findings (by Hull, Miller, Spence, and other students of the subject). Petrazycki's learning theory explains the emergence of drives; physiologically useful drives appear, spread (and get inherited) as an adjustive response to needs of animal or human organisms; attractive drives are evoked by positive, aversive drives by negative, reinforcers. Socially useful drives directed toward or against various kinds of human behavior become evoked by the respective benefits and disadvantages of the behavior for the social group. Thus the drives, biological and social, emerge in the process of "operant conditioning" (as it would be called today), and Petrazycki discovered the process independently of Pavlov, and many decades before Skinner. Moreover, he avoided the one-sidedness of the latter and of many other instrumental learning theorists by emphasizing the role of cognitive processes. Human subjects inform one another of reinforcing events which follow various kinds of behavior, and images of the events—of benefits and disadvantages, rewards and punishments—become reinforcers themselves. The notion provides a foundation for the theory of ethical education by lawmakers: images of legal sanctions spread among members of the social group, and, reinforcing their legal drives, become tools for instrumental learning.

After these general comments, some elements of Petrazycki's system may be presented in more detail. We will be proceeding from more to less general components. Thus, a note on his theory of science, in particular on the adequacy of theories, will go first, followed by sociology, and, subsequently, by legal (and moral) theory. Social engineering through law—a specific, practical outcome of the system—will close the book. All the elements will be dealt with against the background of more recent developments in the respective fields. In particular, Petrazycki's sociology will be presented in the light of structural-functional and interactionist perspectives, and jurisprudence from the perspective of realist and neorealist doctrines.

This will be a critical presentation. Petrazycki's is a controversial system, as even this brief introduction should make clear. The idea of adequacy of theories, if taken literally, may be considered as too demanding to promote the development of scientific knowledge, in particular of the behavioral sciences. Introspective psychology would be opposed by many. The notion of a social evolution progressing toward the ideal of human perfection may be considered as historically unfounded, and the ideal itself as utopian. Moreover, reducing the ultimate social goods to one value, even as lofty as loving one's neighbor, may be challenged by those who favor a pluralistic and open society. Petrazycki's antinormative approach—his rejection of norms as a conceivable subject of legal (and moral) theory, and their replacement with experiences—is particularly controversial. Petrazycki accepts the approach for two reasons: his requirement for adequacy of theories, and for their fertility. The latter demand is undoubtedly and fully legitimate. However, does it justify the antinormative stand? True, from the fertility viewpoint, it would be difficult to argue against a theory of legal experiences, that is, psychology of law, and the very work of Petrazycki corroborates this. Nevertheless, the viability of legal psychology does not necessarily preclude fertile theorizing on legal norms as well. (Petrazycki himself does not completely reject norms from the language of his system; in particular, when speaking about law as a tool for engineering, he clearly has legal norms in mind, not experiences.) Finally, the fact that both legal norms and experiences may be considered as the legitimate subject for theories does not settle the semantic question of which of them are to be called "law." One may argue, contrary to Petrazycki's stipulation, for reserving the name for the former, and accepting another term, such as the German *Rechtsgefühl*, to denote the latter.

Petrazycki's genius, the originality of his views, and the consistency of his system, his optimistic faith in the feasibility of social progress and in the use of reason to promote it, will, hopefully, be evident to the reader of the following chapters. However, any theory can prove its viability only if exposed to severe criticism, which is why a critical attitude has been adopted by the contributors. The analysis which follows will clearly expose the weaknesses and strengths of Petrazycki's philosophy. Some of his contentions will have to be rejected or modified as too extreme, while others will prove themselves. Those which are proven and modified should enhance the development of behavioral science, and thus become a lasting contribution to our knowledge of man in society.

[1]On Petrazycki's life see, for example, Nicholas S. Timasheff, "Introduction," *Law and Morality: Leon Petrazycki*, trans. Hugh W. Babb (Cambridge, Mass.: Harvard University Press, 1955), pp. XXI-XXXI; Georges S. Langrod and Michalina Vaughan, "The Polish Psychological Theory of Law," W. J. Wagner, ed., *Polish Law throughout the Ages* (Stanford, Calif.: Hoover Institution Press, 1970), pp. 306-315.

[2]Petrazycki's views on theory of science were offered in: *Vvedeniie v izucheniie prava i nravstvennosti* (Introduction to the Study of Law and Morality) (3rd ed.; St. Petersburg: J. N. Erlich, 1908), pp. 38-112; *Law and Morality*, pp. 17-21; see also *Nowe podstawy logiki i klasyfikacji umiejetnosci* (New Foundations of Logic and Classification of Sciences) (Warszawa: Wyd. im Petrazyckiego, 1939).

[3]Petrazycki, *Teoriia prava i gosudarstva v sviazi s teoriei nravstvennosti* (Theory of Law and State in Connection with a Theory of Morality) (2nd ed.; St. Petersburg, Ekateringofskoe Pechatnoe Delo, 1909-10), vol. 1, pp. 262-285.

[4]On Petrazycki's psychology see his: *O motivakh chelovicheskikh postupkov* (On the Motives of Human Behavior) (St. Petersburg: E. L. Prokhovshchikov, 1904); *Vvedeniie*, pp. 30-37, 115-265; *Teoriia*, vol. 1, pp. 1-49; *Law and Morality*, pp. 12-17, 22-45.

[5]Of course, images of courage or cowardice may arouse not only aesthetic, but also ethical, experiences; an analysis of the latter follows.

[6]See Petrazycki's *Vvedeniie*, pp. 23-29; *Teoriia*, vol. 1, pp. 30-134; *Law and Morality*, pp. 6-12, 35-88.

[7]See Petrazycki's *Teoriia*, vol. 1, pp. 145-146; *Law and Morality*, p. 95.

[8]See Petrazycki's *Teoriia*, vol. 1, pp. 222-238; *Law and Morality*, pp. 140-148.

[9]On the distinction and its corollaries see Petrazycki's *Teoriia*, vol. 2, pp. 472-528; *Law and Morality*, pp. 221-253.

[10]This distinction enabled Petrazycki to identify justice in a new manner. The term must not be reified: there do not exist any objective characteristics of just persons or just behavior. Instead, the term denotes a feeling of "what is due to whom" within the field of "distribution of rewards and punishments, of goods and burdens"; a feeling being experienced "not on the ground of statutes . . . but according to our 'conscience'—our autonomous views independent of any outside authorities" (*Teoriia*, vol. 2, p. 508). Of course, thus understood, justice means impulsions of intuitive law; more precisely, impulsions of intuitive law referring to acts or to the character of those in power who distribute goods and rewards, punishments and burdens.

[11]On the theory of revolution see Petrazycki's *Teoriia*, vol. 2, pp. 497-500; *Law and Morality*, pp. 235-237.

[12]See Petrazycki's *Teoriia*, vol. 1, pp. 196-217; *Law and Morality*, pp. 128-137.

[13]See Petrazycki's *Teoriia*, vol. 1, pp. 184-196; *Law and Morality*, pp. 120-128.

[14]Petrazycki, *Teoriia*, vol. 1, p. 186.

[15]*Ibid.*

[16]See *ibid.*, vol. 2, pp. 746-758; *Law and Morality*, pp. 324-330; *O ideale spolecznym i odrodzeniu prawa naturalnego* (Social Ideal and Revival of Natural Law) (Warszawa: L. Idzikowski, 1925).

[17]Petrazycki presented his views on the social role of universities in *Universitet i nauka* (The University and Science) (St. Petersburg, 1907). See also Langrod and Vaughan, "Polish Psychological Theory," pp. 325-327, esp. note 107.

[18]See, in particular, Petrazycki's: *Die Lehre vom Einkommen*, vol. 2 Berlin: Verlag von H. W. Muller, 1895), pp. 437-628; "Vvedeniie v nauku politiki prava" (Introduction to the Science of Legal Policy), *Universitetskaiia Isvestiia*, 8-10 (1896-1897), pp. 1-250; *Vvedeniie*, pp. 1-8.

CHAPTER

2

The Concept of Adequate Theory

TADEUSZ KOTARBIŃSKI

Leon Petrazycki's concept of adequate theory was, to me, his most attractive and interesting idea.[1] His point can best be recalled if we start from the example which he himself willingly had been using. The example, unscientific as it seems at first glance, is in fact scientifically convincing. Suppose that a person is interested in the laws of gravitation and makes the statement that all cigars, if neither supported nor suspended, fall. Obviously, such a statement would be as it were lame, insufficient, even though it is true that a cigar falls if it is neither supported nor suspended, because it follows the laws of gravitation. The defect of the statement under consideration does not consist in the choice of the example, which may be intentionally trivial; nor is it due to the falsehood of the statement, because the statement *is* true. It must accordingly be due to something else. Now the statement that an object falls if it is neither supported nor suspended applies not only to cigars but to all physical bodies in general. What is the issue then? If we wish to make general statements which would be scientific in nature, then it does not suffice that what is predicated in a given statement be true about those objects about which the statement is made: such a statement ought to cover all those objects concerning which it is true. This is the gist of the requirement for the adequacy of statements, that is, the requirement that general statements must come up to facts. A general statement ought to cover all the objects to which the predicate applies, and not selected objects only. Petrazycki called general theories which refer to only some objects out of those which are covered by a given predicate "lame," because they resemble a person who leans on one leg alone, although he can stand on both. And if a theory covers not only those objects to which a given predicate in fact applies, but also those to which a given predicate does not apply, then the resulting statement is false. But the result is not merely false: such a theory (which in Petrazycki's odd terminology is called "jumping") tries to find support where it cannot find it. Should a person, for instance, state not only about physical bodies that they fall if they are neither supported nor suspended, but would extend his statement so as to cover with it numbers, mental states, and so on, by saying that they fall if they are neither supported nor suspended, his statement would be entirely inappropriate, because the predicate would cover something to which it is not applicable. Such a statement would be inadequate and would deserve to be called "jumping."

Suppose now that it is quite clear what those methodologists who would like scientific statements to be adequate require. To put it briefly, a general statement is adequate if it ascribes a certain property to all and only those objects which do have it.

I used to be interested in these issues because of my interest in the history of logic and methodology. And here I have found something which I did not in the least expect. Petrazycki had worked out his idea of adequate theories himself, and there is no reason to believe that he could have known anything about his predecessors. Yet it turns out that his idea has had a clear ancestry in the history of methodology and goes back to Aristotle. Aristotle, obviously, did not refer to cigars, but to triangles. He wrote that, should a person state that every equilateral triangle has the sum of its inner angles equal to that of two right angles, then his theory would be inadequate, because it would refer to equilateral triangles only, whereas it holds for a much broader class of objects: we may truly state about any triangle that the sum of its inner angles equals that of two right angles. This is why only the statement which says that every triangle has the sum of its inner angles equal to that of two right angles is adequate.

Aristotle used to ascribe great importance to the adequacy of theories: he emphasized that only adequate theories indicate the direction of a causal or logical nexus. For, if we analyze in detail the concept of triangle as such, then we arrive at the conclusion that all triangles share the property of having the sum of the inner angles equal to that of two right angles. That property, however, cannot be deduced from the fact that some triangles are rectangular. Such was Aristotle's idea, which he discussed at some length in *Posterior Analytics.*

The idea was not taken up for a long time, until Aristotle's concept of adequate theories was recalled in the sixteenth century by Petrus Ramus, and the issue again became a living one. But even before that time, if we recede into the past once more, we find that Alexander of Aphrodisias, a commentator on Aristotle's works, coined certain terms which semantically, even though not philosophically, corresponded to those names of inadequate theories which came to be propagated by Petrazycki. Alexander concentrated on the positive aspects of theories: a theory which does not deserve to be blamed for its "lameness" (in Petrazycki's terminology) he called "free from omissions," and a theory which does not refer to objects to which a given predicate does not apply and which thus does not deserve to be blamed (in Petrazycki's terminology) as "jumping" he called "free from transgressions." His corresponding Greek terms were: *anellipos, aperittos, apartizontos* (adequately). The terminology is inessential; the important point is that there had been certain words which corresponded to an adequate theory as opposed to inadequate ones.

Ramus took up all the distinctions made by Aristotle (without, however, referring to Alexander's terminology); after Ramus it was Francis Bacon, who referred to Aristotle. This was so because Bacon was interested in propagating the idea of adequate theories in connection with his search for relationships which would enable inventions with fairly broad applicability to be made. If an invention—a machine or a chemical method—is to have general applicability it must be based on adequate theorem, and this was why Bacon looked for hints in the past. By the way, he wrote about that in one of his least known and least read works, which bears the mysterious title of *Valerius Terminus.* But these things are now known to those British scholars who have studied Bacon's biography and his works.

Here the tradition breaks. After Bacon, people stopped mentioning adequate theories. Petrazycki took up the issue from scratch as a result of his interest in legal theory. He was thus interested neither in geometry (like Aristotle), nor in the proper classification of domains of sciences (which was the point stressed by Ramus), nor in inventions. Petrazycki was interested in finding theoretical generalizations which could be used in his analysis of the theory and the applications of law, in basing legal policy on appropriate relationships.

Such is, as it seems, the balance sheet of the past: a rediscovery of a problem which had been raised long ago and came to be forgotten long ago, and yet has been vital all the time. I have tried to write about these things in various ways. Recent years saw the publication of a commemorative book dedicated to Philip Merlan, a philologist and a great lover of classical antiquity (who had been born near Lvov, and became a professor at Clermont). When he died some years ago, his friends issued a book entitled *Philomathes* (a lover of knowledge), as Merlan was called by his friends. The book includes my contribution, "Petrazycki's Concept of Adequate Theorem in the Light of Earlier Related Doctrines";[2] the text had been previously published in Polish in a Petrazycki commemorative book.[3]

To conclude, I wish to make some comments not about the past, but about some consequences of the concept of adequate theories. I am personally very much interested in the construction of praxiology as the theory of positive and negative recommendations concerned with efficient action, a theory which would be applicable to all human arts and occupations. I am concerned with such an approach because the recommendations offered by management science are in most cases formulated inadequately, since they refer to business management only, whereas they ought to cover all kinds of organized action.

Thus, when we try to single out general praxiological recommendations out of those with which management science is concerned, we return to the issue of singling out adequate praxiological statements, and this is why I have referred to Petrazycki's theory in order to use it in this connection. This is presumably how a disciple may show his gratitude to his teacher.

But some reservations must be made here. First, Petrazycki formulated the issue as if adequacy were obligatory in the case of all scientific statements. That is certainly an exaggeration. Moreover, his analysis was concerned only with the statements of the type "all A's are B's," whereas in fact this is only one of the numerous types of general scientific statements.[4] Second, satisfying certain conditions of optimality and satisfying the condition of being scientific at a certain stage in the development of science are two different things. Laws which are applicable to entire classes of objects often emerge out of partial laws, which are therefore "lame," since they ascribe a given property to only some objects of that class. For instance, the general laws of genetics were first established with reference to certain plant species only.

Finally, one marginal comment. Petrazycki's point was to single out classes of objectively homogeneous objects, and not of eclectically selected conglomerates, because in his opinion adequate scientific statements can be made only about homogeneous classes. Constructing a scientific theory of "game" or "spices" would end in failure, even though these two terms are very useful when it comes to hunting and cooking, respectively. Hence he warned against the method of constructing classes of objects by covering with a single term as objectively homogeneous all that and only that which in ordinary parlance is covered by one and the same term. A person who would try to construct a homogeneous class by combining into a whole all that which is covered by the term "law" would find himself in a trap (in Polish *prawo* is even more comprehensive than the English term *law*, as it covers the meaning of *right* as well). This is so because "law" is an ambiguous term, and each of its meanings has its counterpart in a different homogeneous class. It is worth noting that in this respect, too, Petrazycki had his predecessor in Aristotle, for the latter also warned against the illusion of looking for something common to all that which is covered by one and the same term. Thus, for instance, it would be wrong to refer to magnanimity as something homogeneous: Alcibiades and Achilles were called magnanimous because they did not tolerate insults, whereas Socrates and Lysander were so called because they did not rebel against adversities and misfortunes.[5] These were, in fact, valuable recommendations and warnings, for even today we witness endeavors to arrive at the essence of morality by searching for what is common to the various uses of the term "morality." People who find nothing that is specifically common to all the uses of that term become, without any good reason, nihilistic about the constants which underlie ethics.

[1]See Leon Petrazycki, *Wstep do nauki prawa i moralnosci* (Introduction to the Study of Law and Morality), trans. Jerzy Lande (Warszawa: Panstwowe Wydawnictwo Naukowe [P.W.N.], 1959), pp. 178-207.

[2]See *Philomathes*, Studies and Essays in the Humanities in Memory of Philip Merlan, R. B. Palmer and R. Hamerton-Kelly, eds. (Netherlands: The Hague, 1971), pp. 350-370.

[3]See K. Opałek, ed., *Z zagadnien teorii prawa i teorii nauki Leona Petrazyckiego. Studia opracowane dla upamietnienia stulecia narodzin* (Selected Issues in Leon Petrazycki's Theory of Law and Theory of Science) (Warszawa: P.W.N., 1969), pp. 29-39. Studies published to commemorate the centennary of his birth.

[4]Compare Władysław Krajewski, "Projekt klasyfikacji praw nauki" (Suggestions for Classification of the Laws of Science), in *Zagadnienia naukoznawstwa*, VIII (1972), 3-31.

[5]Aristotle, *Posterior Analytics*, II, 13, 97815.

CHAPTER

3

The Sociology of Petrazycki[1]

JERZY LANDE

Translated by John W. Slawikowski

Petrazycki's sociology is not widely known. His consistent and comprehensive theoretical system encompasses a wide range of humanistic and social disciplines. These are logic and methodology, psychology, the theories of law and of morality, as well as general hints toward a theory of ethics, language, religion, and so forth. The final culmination of all these efforts is sociology, which results from the development of theories about law and morality.

Petrazycki had promised for a long time to publish a separate work presenting his sociology. When, in 1919, he settled in Warsaw, he accepted a chair of sociology at the Warsaw Law School, a position established at his request. He lectured on sociology several times, but he did not publish the work. He had three manuscripts of sociology, each written at a different time. The last copy was written in Warsaw. However, poor health and depression prevented him from finishing the book and publishing it.

Rafal Wundheiler, one of Petrazycki's students, initiated an abridged presentation of Petrazycki's sociology. Since he had in his possession notes from several years of Petrazycki's lectures, he read them back to Petrazycki, who then corrected and completed the notes. In this manner he worked out the shortened text. He omitted much of the specific material, but in general covered the whole field. The text should have been published immediately, but Petrazycki kept putting it off until his death. Petrazycki's widow retained the handwritten copies of the Sociology as well as many other notes, texts, and the typescript edited by Wundheiler. However, the 1944 Warsaw uprising led to the complete destruction of these documents. The Sociology in its original form was lost forever.

The Social Function of Law

According to Petrazycki, law can be analyzed on two levels: (1) as a real phenomenon; (2) as a norm, that is, on a logical level of inquiry. The latter is where various legal disciplines work, like civil or criminal law; they are concerned with systematizing and interpreting law as norms in force. Petrazycki considers the first of the two levels as more important for scientific inquiry, and rightly so. The question he entertains (in paragraphs two and three of the *Introduction to the Study of Law and Morality*) is: In what sphere does law exist as a real phenomenon? The answer given: It is in the mind of that person who experiences legal judgment. The conclusion is that it is only possible to examine this phenomenon by psychological methods: by introspection and by observation of human behavior. The application of these methods is shown in the *Theory of Law and State*, and in the essay *On the Motives of Human Behavior.*

Petrazycki defines legal experiences as one kind of ethical experience (that is, experience of obligation). The legal experience is bilateral: it combines both obligation and claim. The other kind, the moral experience, is one-sided: it is limited to the obligation only. If we conceive some behavior, like cash payment, as our obligation, and, at the same time, as another person's claim, the experience is legal; for example, paying rent to a landlord. If, on the other hand, we conceive a behavior as our duty, the fulfillment of which cannot be claimed by any other person, the experience is moral; for example, almsgiving to a beggar.

The legal tradition sees the social function of law primarily in terms of court decisions. Petrazycki maintains that court decisions play a secondary role. Dealing with conflicts which result from the inefficient working of the law, decisions are pronounced in pathological situations only. Efficient working of the law brings orderly, that is, conflictless behavior, and this is its basic function. The function is due both to the motivational impact of law (providing a stimulus toward required behavior), and to its educative impact (instilling permanent dispositions into the human mind). The social function of law is, according to Petrazycki, an outcome of its purely psychological impact on the attitudes of individuals. That is why I will present, very briefly, the psychological impact first.

(1) While morality produces only obligational motives toward others, the law produces an "active" feeling of one's rights. Consequently, it shapes human dignity and creates a citizen, in contrast to a slave who does not have any rights; sometimes an excess of this attitude brings about barratry, or the taking advantage of ascriptive privileges.

(2) A feeling of legal obligation produces a stronger pressure, because it implies awareness that the other party has a right to have his claim fulfilled. (Attached to this are aiding motives, like the fear of sanction, and so on.) That is why law, although it is not as highly valued as morality, is a more important social factor: it evokes uniform behavior, while morality is somewhat of a luxury. (Petrazycki compares morality and law to champagne and water, respectively.) This, however, does not mean that morality is socially worthless: (a) Morality emerges ordinarily in the role of a forerunner. New progressive ethical views arise ordinarily as moral ideas, in order to be only gradually transformed into legal ideas. (b) Next to law, morality plays a valuable role. It complements law. It gives men incentives to fulfill more than their ordinary obligations. It takes the rough edges off the routine and rigidity of law. (In these few lines I have summarized the essay *On the Motives of Human Behavior.*)

(3) The moral attitude concentrates its attention and appraisal on the subject of obligation. Hence, there is a tendency to require the fulfillment of the obligation by the subject himself, and to require that it be fulfilled consciously, as an obligation. On the other hand, a legal attitude focuses on the claim and its subject, and, consequently, it often tends to pay off because of "outside" motives (interest, compulsion), or even through other persons (a father on behalf of his child, a friend on behalf of a debtor). It is on this basis that an inaccurate theory arose about the "internal," psychic character of morality, and about the impact of law affecting external human behavior only.

(4) In the case where one does not fulfill his obligations, morality limits itself to grievance or rebuke. The legal attitude, as a result of its "active" character (see above, point 1), is prone to claim and to enforce. (This difference gave rise to inaccurate theories about compulsion as the peculiar characteristic of law.) Thus, morality has a more mellow and peaceful character. Law, on the other hand, has belligerent tendencies. In the presence of the incompatibility of existing views it leads to conflicts (for example, the conviction of two nations that each has rights to the same territory is a powerful incentive to fighting war).

(5) Law is a psychic phenomenon, and therefore the contents of legal experiences (who owes what to whom) of different persons can vary.

Consequently, and due also to the "belligerent" character of law, there can arise conflicts among people. Yet certain social processes bring about a unifying tendency which leads in social groups to a uniformity of the contents of legal experiences. Because of the bilateral nature of law, this uniformity also implies congruity: for instance, one member of the group imputes the right of political power to himself, while all the others consider it their duty to obey him. The unifying tendency flows through three channels: (a) Law, to a greater degree than morality or language, becomes positive, that is, based upon norm-making processes which are viewed as binding by the general population. Today these are mainly legislative processes, with their enactment and enforcement apparatus; however, history indicates that during the times when this apparatus did not function the spontaneous trend was to base law upon the patterns at hand. An example would be the reception of Roman law in medieval times, or the promoting of collections, and even private projects, to the status of legal sources. The legal profession participates in this process by filling the gaps and smoothing out the inconsistencies within the system. This explains the persistence with which lawyers limit the term "law" to official law only, and with which they believe in the unity of official law. (b) While morality formulates its obligations in a very flexible manner—for example, the obligation of charitable acts ranges from giving a poor man a dime to depriving oneself of all one's assets—law aspires to a complete specification of what ought to be done, of the conditions for fulfillment, and so on. For example, one becomes of legal age on a specified day, and a levied tax amounts to a definite sum and is payable at a specified moment. Such a pattern at times runs contrary to the facts. People attain, in different degrees and at different ages, the ability to command themselves and their resources. However, a set law prevents controversies and conflicts. (c) When a disagreement occurs despite all efforts to avert it, people have a tendency to place the dispute before the discretion of a third, neutral party. (Hence, the institution of courts; today they are scrupulously regulated and richly differentiated, but hark back to the most primitive social systems.)

Of course, the above statements refer not only to the individual but also to social processes. However, Petrazycki begins to speak explicitly about the social function of law only when he introduces a new issue—coordinated interaction in social groups. Homogeneous and coordinated (due to the unifying tendency), legal experiences elicit in each social group a suitable system of mutual behavior which is itself homogeneous and coordinated. Petrazycki discerns two different social functions of law: the distributive, controlling the distribution and the circulation of goods, and the organizational, establishing the structure of groups. The first produces the economic system; the second, the political system, especially the state.

The distributive function is based on the widespread working of incentives related to the norms of private law. Experiencing the right of property implies, first, ascribing to someone A the right to control the object and to prevent anybody else from interfering with the object; and second, ascribing to all others besides A the obligation to accept A's control, and to not interfere. The process of unification brings about a homogeneous outlook on mutually accepted rights and obligations within the group. This results in the emergence of a coordinated system of behavior of group members with respect to goods on the market: person A utilizes his rights (for example, to live in his house, to mortgage, lease, or sell it), and others accept his behavior and do not interfere. Principles of the law of contracts work alike, bringing about the coordination of behavior of the contracting parties (debtors repay, creditors accept). The same is true with respect to family law and the law of inheritance. Legal motives are here the basic factor, but not the only one. The fear of sanction provides an additional motivation. The relative force of both differs markedly: a solid citizen respects the property of others "as a principle," while a thief refrains from a theft if the risk of apprehension is too high.

Private law incentives induce people to fulfill only those actions which are prescribed by the norms in force; for example, the property owner exercises his right to exclusive possession and defends his property against the infringement of others. The law does not delegate him any other functions. In fact, however, owners usually assume many other activities not specified by law. Owners take care to maintain their property in good condition. They seek profit by leasing it, by using it as a security, or by selling it. Here, then, emerges another, independent motivation—to avoid losses and to attain gains. This very motivation induces men, on the basis of the law of contracts, to enter contracts, to buy cheap and to sell high, to make profitable credit transactions, and so on; and it induces them, on the ground of family and inheritance laws, to amass property exceeding their own needs in order to insure an adequate living to their families before and after their deaths. The uniform functioning of the norms of private law lays the foundation for these actions. It makes everyone expect that the contracting parties will fulfill their obligations, and that third parties will not infringe upon people's rights; this is why, in times of war or disorder, that economic activity dwindles when expectations are perceived to be unfounded. The functioning of these norms, that is, the working of a uniform system of behavior, is the basis for another uniform behavioral system—the economic system, the subject of inquiry of political economy.

Petrazycki builds his theory of the political system as an outcome of the organizational function of law in a way similar to the analysis of the economic system as an effect of the distributive function. The starting point here is the phenomenon of authority. Authority as a psychic event is a legal experience composed of two legal relationships; first, a person in power has the right to command (that is, to expect the fulfillment of certain acts), matched by the obligation to obey requests. Second, he has the right to interfere in the personal affairs of a subordinate, for example, to punish him, matched by an obligation on the subordinate's part of yielding to his interference. Here again, the processes of unification and coordination bring about consensus among individual members of the group. Consequently, a system of behavior emerges which is directed by legal and auxiliary motives: men obey those in power within the respective limits of their authority, and the powerholders command and interfere within these limits. In the course of development there occurs a differentiation of powers. There are general authorities with a broad range of powers (father, the state), and specific authorities (judge, teacher); "lordlike" authorities who give orders in their own interest (slaveowner toward his slave, businessman toward his employee), and those providing social service, that is, an obligation to care for the welfare of their subordinates (father, teacher, the state). Finally, together with the specialization of powers, there emerges a hierarchical structure: a lower level powerholder is obliged to obey his higher-ups, sometimes throughout a long line of command. Uniform behavior—following directives of common authorities—produces division into groups. In more complex societies these groups intersect. Nevertheless, they make a structured system which culminates in submission to a common sovereign authority. Such an authority can knit a kinship group or an apparent kinship group (patriarchal family systems) together, or it can depend exclusively upon legal bonds: in the latter case we deal with an official group, that is, the state. Group cohesion increases due to the legal incentives of authority and the auxiliary incentives, as well as to numerous other incentives which influence mutual behavior; some of these are the obligations of powerholders to serve the good of their subordinates and the respective rights of the latter, a feeling of solidarity, the bonds of a common culture, language, and so on.

The Sociology of Petrazycki[2]

Sociology cannot be a theory "of society," nor can it be a theory of everything which is social, since both of these are intricate conglomerates of various multifactorial phenomena. In order to be scientific (that is, adequate), sociology must choose for itself a particular subject on which one may predicate peculiar truths. The subject is "the social process," understood as changes in individual and group experiences, and in social behavior, which occur in the course of adaptation. With some reservations, sociology may be called the theory of social development or of the development of culture. So conceived, it will be located on the level of generality immediately higher than the theory of the origin and the development of law, morality, state, language, religion, and so on.

Darwinism demonstrated that adaptation is being reached through small, hereditary changes which enable some individuals and species to survive. This thesis, which is applicable for all forms of life, is also relevant to social life: groups less adapted perish in the struggle (for example, the Polish state disappeared in the eighteenth century). However, this thesis does not provide a full explanation of the social process; it does not explain the rapid (if conditions change) emergence, in animals and in humans, of impulses toward individually advantageous behavior. Moreover, if social progress depended only upon the struggle for existence, it would be very slow, and progress would be achieved at the cost of a continual extermination of large human groups—which has not been the case in the history of mankind.

In law and morality, which constitute values directing our behavior and our dispositions toward others, changes sometimes occur quickly and on a large scale (I mean here societies standing at a certain level of development, and not in a state of stagnation). There is, in particular, one basic tendency in the process of law formation and development: the contents of legal experiences (and their motivating and educative influence) become adapted to existing group attitudes in such a manner that the system of law directs the attitudes and behavior of men toward the good of the group. Consequently, as common attitudes become better adapted to the social life the law itself changes as well. The changes in law run in accord with the following three tendencies.

(1) The tendency of increased demands. Every consecutive system of law demands from men more, as far as socially rational behavior is concerned. For instance, the inventory of forbidden behavior increases through time, from brief lists of offenses in primitive groups to the comprehensive catalogs of criminal, and administrative, and other offenses

which are known to contemporary laws. The same occurs in the field of required positive acts. It is also true for individual crimes: for example, the prohibition of homicide initially refers to persons of the same or higher status (killing slaves and even one's own children is permitted), and to the members of one's own group (killing a stranger is seen as meritorious). Later the prohibition is stretched to include strangers and even assailants (the use of excessive force in self-defense). The demands increase not only numerically but also qualitatively: compare the duty of parents for educating their children two hundred years ago, and today. This increase in demands becomes possible because men, under the influence of social training, become more and more capable of compliance.

(2) The tendency to change incentives. At more advanced levels of social development, the law produces indentical behavior by the use of higher incentives. Thus, it utilizes advances in the gradual socialization of men. The higher ranking of an incentive is understood here not ethically, but teleologically, as its greater efficiency. The consecutive social systems are here an instance. All of them have at least one purpose in common: to persuade men to work. However, the system of serfdom is based on the very primitive motive of fear of physical force. It was succeeded by the individualist system: here, productive work is not compulsory, but motivated by the expectation of gain and security, both for oneself and one's family. This system can work only at those levels of social development where men have achieved the capacity for independent planning, inventiveness, and an inclination to work. The next level, the socialist order, replaces these motives of private rivalry by the motives of duty and the social good. Parallel changes occur within political structures. After the despotic phase, based on fear, there emerges a liberal system reaching its summit in parliamentary democracy; it is based on individual freedom, competition between individuals, and on competition between groups formed freely by individuals. It is characterized by the spirit of mutual mistrust: the citizen vests authority only in those elected by himself, and in extreme cases he trusts no one, but directly operates the government and the administration of justice (Athenian democracy and the ideal of Rousseau). Today (let it be remembered that Petrazycki said this during the period from 1906 to 1910) there occur signs of a return to centralism, to a system based on governments run by specialists. While important democratic achievements are maintained (a representative government, elected and checked by the population), men are apt to place their trust not upon elected party politicians but on qualified specialists. Hence parliamentary appointments, delegations of power, the growing importance of ex-

pert committees at the expense of plenary parliamentary sessions. (Totalitarian systems could probably be considered as pathological outgrowths of this trend, in conjunction with certain reactionary tendencies.)

(3) The tendency to diminish motivational pressure. In the process of social development, motivation of the same kind brings socially demanded behavior with the aid of ever diminishing pressure. This can be illustrated by the decrease of rewards through time. In the Middle Ages, the rulers of provinces had to be encouraged by being given ownership of territory. Later on, they were paid by high honors and income. In contemporary democracies the top-ranking officials receive a modest monetary reward and their life style differs little from that of the "common man." Similarly, punishments become less severe, from the initial cruel punishments (torture, collective responsibility) to the humaneness of today. The same occurs with regard to sanctions of private law. In order to compel the debtor to pay his debt, the early Roman law threatened him with "being cut up into pieces," and as late as the nineteenth century he was threatened with jail. Today, a threat to pay interest or damages is sufficient to induce compliance.

Of course, these tendencies are realized in full only where there are no counteracting factors; and we can discover these tendencies at work only within the development of a particular culture. The history of the ancient world (Greece and the Roman Empire) can be conceived as a more or less consistent evolution. However, the absorption by Rome of the barbarian masses led to a cultural decline and resulted in retrogressive evolution, culminating in the complete breakdown of Roman culture. The new Romanic-Germanic-Slavic nations thus began their development from infancy, and have continued to advance since then. However, their unequal development, and the ease of cultural borrowing from the most advanced among them, has sometimes had unfavorable effects. Nevertheless, even the soundest development is not rectilinear: every new system once produced by the above tendency to change incentives increases originally the pressures of some incentives in order to later decrease the pressure when the incentives already work well, and when reduced coercion is sufficient to achieve suitable behavior of the masses. For example, in the beginnings of the individualist system a serious threat of hunger and the temptation for unlimited wealth are present; but soon, even before socialistic reforms, the hunger pressure mellows (limitation of working hours, prohibition of child labor), and unlimited growth of individual wealth becomes prevented by progressive income taxes.

Petrazycki here then presents a theory of social progress. The theory is not complete, because it only deals with the development of law (it is also relevant to morality), but, due to the prominent role of law in society, it explains a lot. Today, scientific knowledge predominantly rejects the idea of progressive social development. Various reasons are being given for the rejection, in particular that the assumption of development to something better presupposes the acceptance of absolute values as criteria of progress. We saw that Petrazycki does not argue this way: he only employs criteria of teleology which, though unknown to men, work objectively in the very process of development. The emphasis he places on the irrational, impulsive character of experiences which determine human behavior, and on the unconscious, nonintentional character of teleology in the process of adjustment, differentiates his theory from the earlier intellectualistic doctrines which believed in progress as an outcome of the development of reason and understanding (Condorcet and Comte). The very theory of development easily explains today's antidevelopmental attitude.[3] The belief in progress characterizes the systems just emerging in the struggle or enjoying their first victories; this is why the belief is present, for example, in the beginnings of the individualist system. When, however, that system disintegrates, there occurs a mood of discouragement and negativism, and scholars see only cyclical occurrences in history, oscillatory movements, or even an oncoming road to disaster. This is also why the idea of progress today is voiced solely by socialist scholars, and its only more profound and consistent theory is, beyond the generally unknown notion of Petrazycki, the Marxist doctrine.

The theory of social progress is not only theoretically valuable as a recognition of real processes; its practical utility is also great, since it is the necessary basis for scientific social policy. That is why Petrazycki makes use of the theory in all the policy considerations found in his various works (see, for example, his preface to the *Introduction to the Study of Law and Morality*; these considerations were elaborated in *The Social Ideal*, and specifically applied to private law in *Die Lehre vom Einkommen*). The absence of a settled view on evolution and on the sequence of social systems deprives other writers, even outstanding and progressively oriented ones (for example, B. Russell, K. Popper, H. Laski) of any criterion for direction of the intended social changes; and it makes their works products of casual and chaotic intuitive evaluations which are, for the most part, a mixture of liberalism and socialism.

Petrazycki's theory of development of law and morality reveals a puzzling purposefulness which governs the formation of ethical values and determines the direction of their development. This purposefulness is indicated by numerous passages of his works referring to various fields of social life. In the *Introduction to the Study of Law and Morality*, he persistently stresses the adjustment of the emotive impulses of animals and of humans to biological and social purposes; and, since the adjustment has been mostly inherited from distant ancestors, he finds in the impulses various elements which survived from the early periods of berry-picking, hunting, and primitive agriculture. In *Die Lehre vom Einkommen*, Petrazycki stresses that Roman lawyers based their decisions on naive ethical intuitions; they merely said that "this is fair," "this is what ought to be done." Nevertheless, these decisions were made, however unintentionally, in accordance with economic goals and with the progress of the social system. In the work *The Social Ideal*, Petrazycki shows that the naive declarations of Rousseau, Kant, and others about the "legitimacy" of certain principles of the legal system, or about their "conformity with natural law," were unconscious expressions of individualism; and that the subsequent claims for "humanitarian" mitigation of punishments were unconscious expressions of the tendency to diminish motivational pressure.

This puzzling purposefulness is explained, with respect to law, by the sociological theory of the development of law, and with respect to all the products of culture, by general sociology. As already hinted, Petrazycki's sociology refers to Darwinism. Darwinism explains the purposefulness of animal and human behavior by natural selection in the struggle for existence. This view needs serious corrections and supplements. Natural selection explains, and only partially, the adaptation of species (the phylocentric adaptation); that is, variations inherited after ancestors, and fit for the ancestors' general conditions of life, but not necessarily for present-day conditions. However, experience demonstrates that an individual adapts quickly, and egocentrically, to actual conditions. An animal produces within himself impulses which attract him to the useful and turn him away from the harmful. The traditional conception of instincts introduced a new myth: a new unknown Y replaced an unknown X (a crushing criticism of this notion is contained in the *Introduction to the Study of Law and Morality*). Petrazycki explains the puzzle very simply, by the theory of "impulsive induction." The theory assumes that the animal psyche has a tendency to react with aversive impulses to an event which brings pain and annoyance, and with attractive impulses to an event which brings pleasure. The further experience results in reinforcement of the relevant associations, and in a decline of the accidental ones.

A pet dog learns quickly not to dirty the home. The fact that he is beaten for infringement does not fully explain the efficiency of the learning, because the dog does not understand either the causal nexus between his offense and the sanction, or the nexus between his asking to go outside and avoiding punishment. After the punishment, the dog associates a repellent impulse with images of all the elements in the occurrence, both rational (the offense, beating), and irrational (if within his field of vision there was a yellow paper, he will be afraid of that paper and will avoid it; and if the punishment was administered with a folded briefcase, he will be afraid of the briefcase). However, every following experience will weaken the association of the impulse with the accidental elements and strengthen its association with the relevant ones. This process is similar to logical induction, but it works without reasoning.

In men, there occurs a similar process; a child must be burned to learn not to touch fire. Here, however, a new factor appears: the ability to reason. This ability improves adaptation, although "impulsive induction" retains its value for men. When the number of experiences is few we are apt to accept accidental appraisements, like the dog's fear of the folded briefcase; for example, the value of marriage will be appraised differently by two men, one of whom has a happy marriage and the other an unhappy one. On the other hand, people on a low intellectual level, for example, children or barbarians, sometimes amaze us by their ability to commit strikingly purposeful acts, although they do not consciously know the function of these acts. On the basis of a sufficient amount of impulsive experiences, the animal and the man produce appraisements which not only distinguish good from bad but which are also proportional to the respective value of the subject. This unconscious purposefulness is more "brilliant" than that which can be reached by reason, and it is directed toward the individual's good.

The actual subject matter of sociology is, however, social adjustment. Here we deal with a new factor: psychological interaction. With the aid of movements, facial expressions, and especially language, the members of a group transmit to one another not only ideas and judgments but also impulsions. Based on these, they mutually transmit evaluations of things, occurrences, and acts. The impulsions are more "contagious" than the intellectual elements: men speak above all about what makes them happy or sad, about what is "good" or "bad," about the virtues and faults of one's fellow men; an individual's fear or anger infects the crowd, and propels it to panic or to violence. So, by transmitting impulsive evaluations to one another, we turn the group into an enormous laboratory of evaluations within which social experience is utilized. Social experience is much richer than the individual, and it takes into account the more distant effects of our actions which are barely accessible to individual experience; for instance, if a member of a primitive tribe perpetrated an act for the first time, for example, killed another tribesman, took his lamb, and invited friends to a mutton feast, there would occur among various partakers in the feast varying appraisals, critical as well as friendly (for example, in the family of the killer, the guests, those unfriendly to the victim). However, the recurrence of killings will eliminate the appraisals which are not conducive to the good of the group, and will strengthen a sharply critical appraisal—thus the killing of a tribesman will be considered a crime. The killing of a member of another group will quickly produce a positive evaluation, and will be perceived as meritorious. In the course of interaction, individual evaluations undergo a process somewhat similar to the struggle for existence and natural selection: those which are not favorable to the group are eliminated, and only evaluations "resultant" from social experience remain—that is, those which are adequate to the social usefulness or harmfulness of the act, and thus serve the group. This social adaptation, according to Petrazycki, is more "brilliant" than the individual.

The adjustment is oriented toward the good of the group, within which is occurring an intellectual and impulsive interchange. That is why there occurs, within a primitive, isolated group, a closely knit group ethic of internal solidarity and an enmity toward all aliens. However, once exchange relations with neighboring groups arise, the experiential laboratory widens and the neighbors become allies and friends. With the development of intergroup relations, the interchange of experiences and appraisements spreads out, and at the same time the ethic expands, and this eventually results in the idea of a brotherhood of man.

This theory on the origin and adaptation of social values is the foundation of Petrazycki's general sociology. In his lectures which I attended, this general sociology was further narrowed down to the sociology of ethical phenomena, that is, to the theory of the origin and development of law and morality. The idea of the emergence of the "resultant" values clearly explains the peculiarities of ethical experiences. Psychological investigation of these experiences shows that: (1) they have an authoritatively mystic character; they speak to us as if in the name of some higher being. Hence, in the common and philosophers' minds, there exist the peculiar "projective" images deriving the experiences from "conscience," divinity, reason, national spirit, the general will, and so on; (2) these aggregate experiences include both the image of a given behavior and an impulse of obligation. They speak to us "categorically," without reference to any purposeful rationale, and they stand opposed to our other aspirations; thus, they act as if they were "commands" which hamper our freedom. One can explain these characteristics of the ethical experiences by two facts. First, the individual receives values from the society through "social persuasion"; hence, this "voice from outside" of a higher importance. Second, the ethical experiences reflect the "resultant" values which are formed in a group from the collision of innumerable individual values. From such a "resultant" there disappear all the reasons, mainly teleological, which accompany individual values, and there remains only the image of a given deed (for example, killing one's tribesman) and of its criminal character, implying an obligation to refrain from it. Some moral philosophers and sociologists partially approached this conception. For example, Durkheim, in *The Determination of Moral Facts*, gives a very similar psychological analysis of "moral" experiences. He also proclaims the social origin of "morality," but his unclear and inconsistent notion results in a naive reification of society, as if it were a person separate from individuals, with its own mind, capable of giving orders to individuals.

I know Petrazycki's conception only in skeletal form, and I have presented it in brief. Undoubtedly, it was more comprehensively developed in his mind. However, even this brief outline shows a great deal of flexibility, in contrast to the schematic character of various related theories. The working of the collective laboratory in which individuals, who are at the same time doers and receivers of values, participate, may clarify many metaphysical puzzles which plague scientific knowledge, like the problem of the "relationship of the individual to the group" or of "social determinism." Of course, some new value, progressive for a given group and for its stage of development, can occur in an individual mind. This does not mean that the value originated from any "revelation," or, as idealists like M. Scheler or H. Bergson claim, from a mysterious "spirit" or "elan." On the contrary, the appearance of each new value must be prepared by social conditions. If the value is not yet adapted to the conditions and the psychic level of the entire group, then, in the process of social interaction, it will either be extinguished or merely remain in the minds of a small intellectual elite without having wider influence; for example, the ethical ideas of the stoics or of Clement of Alexandria. If, on the other hand, the value is adapted, it will expand and, winning the "referendum," it will be commonly held. Within more differentiated societies we have to take account of more than one, and sometimes of many, "laboratories," like castes or classes, and in strongly antagonistic intergroup conditions class tensions can reach such a degree that the common "resultants" cannot be generated, and the conflict is resolved by revolution.

I have summarized what I know about Petrazycki's sociology. How can his system be classified? To which group does it belong? I believe that "evolutionism" would be the proper label, since the central problem here is social development; and the theory of the maturation of law indicates what important results the author achieved in learning both the roots and the direction of social change.

[1]A translation of "Socjologia Petrazyckiego," *Przeglad Socjologiczny*, 12 (1958), pp. 229-265. (The original contains the following editorial note: "The present article was written in 1948. Having been submitted to *Przeglad Socjologiczny*, it was scheduled for publication in the 1950 volume. However, the volume did not appear. The author, Professor Jerzy Lande, died in Cracow on December 10, 1954.") In this book the article has been edited; in particular, discussion of some misunderstandings on the part of Petrazycki's critics has been omitted. Volumes 1950-1956 of *Przeglad Socjologiczny* did not appear due to a ban on sociological publications in that period of time. (Eds. note.)

[2]From now on I will present the contents of Chapter VI of the *Theory of Law and State*, and supplement it on the ground of other works by Petrazycki and with my notes of his lectures which I attended, in 1906 to 1910, at the University of St. Petersburg.

[3]Compare the criticism and analysis of its intellectual sources in an excellent article by Tadeusz Kotarbiński, published in *Mysl Wspolczesna* (1949), 1-2. (The article, "On Disregarding the Evolutionary Approach in the Methodology of the Humanities," appeared, in English, in Tadeusz Kotarbiński, *Gnosiology: The Scientific Approach to the Theory of Knowledge* [Oxford: Pergamon Press, 1966], pp. 492-498. [Eds. note.])

CHAPTER

4

Petrazycki's Sociology in the Perspective of Structural-Functional Theory

HARRY M. JOHNSON

Petrazycki's Defintion of Law

Definitions of technical terms are always somewhat arbitrary, of course, and beyond a certain point there is no use in arguing about them. They are, however, deeply involved in the theories of their authors, and they do tend to sensitize us to some aspects of reality and perhaps blind us to others. We can understand and "place" Petrazycki's specific conception of law by listing some of the criteria that various writers have regarded as important, either in their definitions or in their subsequent distinctions:

(1) Normativeness. Law is commonly regarded as something having to do with norms of social interaction. This is true for Petrazycki, but he emphasizes, not the norms (to which he attributes some lesser kind of "reality"), but feelings, images, impulses to act ("legal impulsions"). Moreover, he interprets "social" interaction broadly. For example, a "madman's" relation with the devil is "social."

(2) Obligation. From the point of view of any particular individual, a norm may be a kind of neutral object, something merely in his situation or environment, or it may be internalized in his personality so that he himself feels an obligation to conform to it. Petrazycki's conception of law implies, among other things, that legal norms "exist" only to the

extent that people feel a sense of duty, a sense that they ought to do something or refrain from doing something.

(3) Cultural aspect. Most writers, perhaps, regard law as a cultural phenomenon in the sense that the norms involved are shared by some, at least, of the participants in a social-interaction system: the norms, to some appreciable extent, mean the same thing to a plurality of participants. For Petrazycki, however, "law" is not necessarily cultural in this sense. For him, one man's eccentric idea that he has an obligation toward Jones and that Jones has a corresponding right, even though neither Jones nor anyone else feels the same way, is a "legal impulsion"—part of "law."

(4) Type of sanction. In the structural-functional theory of Talcott Parsons, there are four ideal-typical ways for *ego* to gain compliance from *alter*. In Parsons's own words:

> This fourfold classification concerns the alternatives open to any acting unit, conventionally designated as *ego* (though it may be a collectivity), that is seeking to bring about an act (or prevent an undesired one) on the part of another unit, *alter*. It involves two dichotomized axes: (1) whether ego's presumptive conditional output is advantageous or disadvantageous to alter, what I call the difference between positive and negative sanctions; (2) whether the advantage or disadvantage involves a prospective or conditional change in *alter's* action *situation*, independent of his intentions, or concerns his intentions, namely the definition of his goals, specified values, etc., independent of his situation.[1]

One of the four classes of sanctions that result from these two distinctions is called "negative situational." These are disadvantageous changes in alter's situation that ego or someone connected with him brings about on account of alter's undesirable performance or nonperformance. They are a class of punishments—punishments, namely, that, going beyond or adding to a negative change in ego's *attitude* toward alter, change alter's situation in other respects, for example, through his having to pay a fine or submit to imprisonment. Now, "laws" are not necessarily attempts on the part of any particular "ego" to gain compliance (although they may be), but some people would say that "laws" are norms that, among other things, are backed up by negative situational sanctions. Petrazycki recognizes, of course, that negative situational sanctions may well help to gain compliance with legal norms, but he does not define law in such a way that it must by definition be backed up by negative situational sanctions. For Petrazycki, however, law *is* backed up by negative "intentional" sanctions (to refer again to Parsons's classification). For Petrazycki, law consists of or somehow resides in "legal impulsions," and since these involve a sense of obligation to do something (or to refrain), it follows of course that "legal experiences" include the experience of guilt or internal self-punishment for avoidable failure or refusal to carry out the inner imperative of any "legal impulsion." In this sense, negative internal (nonsituational) sanctions of guilt or shame are for Petrazycki the only sanctions that "law" must have by definition. I cannot speak for all "structural-functional" theorists, but certainly for many and, I think, most of them, "law" is an important part of "social structure" because it is to some considerable extent cultural and is backed up by negative situational sanctions. For a modern structural-functional theorist, the rights or claims that are involved in "law" are recognized in a social system of some kind; they live not only in the mind of some possible demented eccentric; they are "enforceable," as we commonly say, in the sense that implies both a certain socially shared feeling that the rights ought to be recognized and implemented and also a realistic possibility that known failure or refusal to comply will be punished by negative situational sanctions. This point holds good for civil law just as much as for criminal, since judicial decisions in civil cases are enforceable. "Law" is social-structural only if it does in fact inform or shape social interaction. This is, of course, a matter of degree.

(5) Creation or source. Some people would restrict the term law to norms that were enunciated or created in the first place by some formal agent or agency to whom or to which someone attributes the right to create binding norms. Such a right, called "authority," is, of course, a matter of degree, both in the sense that the right may be limited in scope and in the sense that perhaps not all people affected recognize its legitimacy. A more elastic criterion would be that, regardless of original source, a norm is "legal" if it has been or would be recognized as binding by someone who *is* authorized to issue binding norms or to interpret them authoritatively. Petrazycki does not restrict "law" in either of these ways.

(6) Functional specialization. Some people would think it not enough that a norm, to be called "legal," be issued or certified by some agent or agency having the right to issue or certify binding norms, but that, in addition, the norm-issuing or -certifying agent or agency must be functionally specialized to some extent specifically as a norm-making or norm-interpreting agency. Thus, in this restricted sense, the norms a father might make for his children are not laws although they might be legitimate informal norms. Similarly, the rules children devise or accept for their games would not be "laws." If children formally established a

club, however, with clearly stated rules, and established a grievance committee and even discretionary negative situational sanctions, we could say (following the criterion of functional specialization) that the club's rules are "legal." The existence of a formal court of some kind that would or might well uphold a given norm in settling disputes authoritatively, meting out negative situational sanctions for infractions, is sometimes treated as a more important criterion of "law" than the existence of a specialized law-making organ. Thus, rules established democratically by all or a majority of ordinary members of a formal organization might be regarded as law even if disputes are also settled formally by the (nonspecialized) body of members as a whole. For Petrazycki, however, all these possibilities, although no doubt important in one way or another, are not defining criteria.

(7) Detection of offenses. An extremely strict definition might require that there be a specialized agency for the detection of violations.

(8) Agency of punishment. An extremely strict definition might also require that there be a specialized agency for carrying out the sentences of the court or courts.

Petrazycki takes account of all these distinctions, but he restricts his definition of law to "imperative-attributive impulsions" (essentially, feelings of obligation, accompanied by the feeling that the content of the obligation is also someone's right). His definition has the great merit of emphasizing the basic element of a subjective sense of obligation. In the long run the "law" is a weak thing unless the people to whom it applies actually feel its normative binding quality within themselves. On the other hand, Petrazycki's definition has at least two grave disadvantages. For a sociologist, "law" is essentially cultural and social, and this fact should perhaps be incorporated in the very definition. Law is a great "code," imperfect no doubt, but sometimes good enough to bind together a whole society by guiding many of its decisions and messages. Petrazycki's definition focuses on the "decisions" and "messages" (his legal impulsions), but it treats as a kind of secondary matter what is in fact basic to the social importance of law, namely, the code aspect—the cultural rules or norms in conformity with which these message-decisions are composed. Second, as Maria Ossowska points out in her paper, the rights or claims in Petrazycki's excessively "psychological" definition are too cloudy to serve as a practical guide to the identification of law. The remedy for this is to treat, as "legal" rights and claims, those that (among other things) are enforceable through the courts and enforcement agencies.

I do not think that Petrazycki is perfectly consistent in keeping to his own definition. To me there are several suggestions that in his mind intuitive law is more truly "law" than positive law, even though formally and strictly both should consist in imperative-attributive impulsions. Petrazycki is so anxious to make the point that law is more than printed characters in books that he sometimes forgets that feelings of obligation can be associated with positive law—in fact, by his definition, must be. First, however, let me recall the fact that the difference between intuitive and positive law, for him, is purely "subjective" in the sense that it depends upon whether the actor whose impulsions we may be talking about does or does not think of "normative facts" in connection with his impulse to carry out a felt obligation, thus implementing someone else's rights. "Normative facts," it will be remembered, include legislative enactments, judges' decisions as precedents, and a variety of other sources of "positive" law. What matters for the distinction between intuitive law and positive law is not whether the subject's impulsion is or is not in fact traceable in part to one or more normative facts; what matters is whether or not he is subjectively aware of being influenced by normative facts. We know this because, for instance, Petrazycki talks not only about the fact that intuitive law may become or be a source of positive law but also about the fact that positive law to which one has become thoroughly habituated may become intuitive law. Petrazycki obviously thinks this latter development is a good thing; and I cannot help feeling, as I have said, that he tends to think of intuitive law as somehow psychologically deeper than positive law. (Insofar as both are law in Petrazycki's sense, I should be inclined to think the opposite, if anything. It seems to me that one is more confident about one's obligations and claims if one feels that they are socially supported. In other contexts, I believe, Petrazycki says something similar.) The point here is that despite his formal definition of law, Petrazycki sometimes implicitly is thinking of positive law as consisting in normative facts. I am not entirely against this, and I intend to argue below that Petrazycki was a kind of structural-functional theorist, but I am saying now that he did not adhere strictly to his own eccentric definition of law.

Another indication of inconsistency is his discussion of conflict between intuitive and positive law. He says: "where their divergence goes beyond certain bounds, the positive law must inevitably break down—and in the case of resistance the debacle will be in the form of a social revolution."[2] It is difficult to see how there could be as deep a conflict as Petrazycki is talking about here between two sets of obligations-and-rights, both felt as such. In this passage, it seems to me, he is using the term "positive law" to refer to what a modern theorist might call uninstitutionalized formal norms. Further, I shall argue below, in this passage the term "intuitive law" comes fairly close to meaning what a modern theorist might call institutionalized societal values. Thus the passage might be interpreted as saying in effect: "Law will tend to be ineffective and alienative if it does not agree with conceptions of what is socially desirable, provided that many people feel these conceptions should be implemented. Attempts to enforce law that is 'illegitimate' in this sense are likely to provoke a revolutionary movement claiming legitimacy in the name of the outraged values."

The same peculiar equivocation occurs, it seems to me, in Petrazycki's definition of justice, which is given in italics. Justice, he says, is achieved when the demands of intuitive law are satisfied. No mention of positive law! Why not? It would seem to be a strange kind of justice that did not take account of people's feelings of obligation and attributions of legitimate rights just because these feelings and attributions happen to be associated with formal enactments of some kind. Petrazycki was, of course, free to define "justice" in any way he liked. My point is that his narrow and eccentric definition probably resulted from his equivocal usage with regard to "positive law." Moreover, his narrow definition probably did not express what he was trying to say. From the context of *Law and Morality* as a whole, I think he meant to say something like the following: "Justice cannot be said to prevail unless existing social relationships and the allocation of rights, responsibilities, and sanctions on the whole agree with widespread social values (conceptions of what should be implemented in the social system), regardless of the source of such values or conceptions."

When Petrazycki talks about the educational function of the law, moreover, he is really talking about the educational function of normative facts. The context makes this quite clear, I think. It is not the law in Petrazycki's strict sense that educates a person to dignity. The dignity of a person *consists* (in part) in the fact (if it is a fact) that in his various social roles he has rights that are recognized by others and are enforceable if necessary.

As I said earlier, it is useless to talk about words beyond a certain point. I think that Petrazycki's occasional inconsistency in the use of his own technical terms reveals subtlety in his thought. His idea in any case is good: that judicial decisions and legislative enactments may help to "educate" the public in the sense of inculcating new obligations and rights. I will take up this topic again below, but first I should like to comment on Petrazycki's distinction between law and morality.

Petrazycki's Distinction between Law and Morality

According to Petrazycki, the difference between law and morality is that law involves both the sense of obligation and the attribution of right, whereas morality involves no attribution of right, only the sense of obligation. This distinction is awkward because it is hard to find a great many obligations that do not involve attributing rights, although it is true, I think, that we tend to call actions moral rather than "legal" when the actor goes beyond what anyone has a "right to expect." Such actions also go "beyond the call of duty," however. The two terms, obligation and right, come very close to implying each other. I should prefer, therefore, to distinguish between law and morality on a different basis. Law consists of norms that, among other things, are backed up by negative situational sanctions as well as attitudes of disapproval, whereas morality consists of values and norms that are backed up certainly by the actor's own negative internal sanctions and possibly by others' attitudes of disapproval, but not by negative situational sanctions in the technical sense. We often make a distinction between "moral" rights and obligations and "enforceable" rights and obligations. This is the distinction I have in mind. If we make this distinction, then not all normative pronouncements even of authorized executives and legislatures are properly called law. Executives and legislatures sometimes exhort people to do this or that (or to refrain) without making compliance mandatory—that is, without providing any negative situational sanctions. This is moral exhortation, not law-making.

I think that this distinction is clearer and more useful than Petrazycki's. If we accepted it, however, we should have to call some of Petrazycki's "laws" moral norms (or "impulsions," if one insists on that term).

The distinction, between law and morality, that is based on the type of sanction involved, corresponds fairly closely, though not precisely, to the distinction that Parsons makes between social-structural norms and social-structural values. Values, as we noted above, are conceptions of what is desirable; and if enough people in a social system accept them as actual standards for structuring the system normatively, then we say that the values are social-structural: The values that people support in this sense (or to which they are "committed," in the stronger sense that they take special responsibility for their implementation) are not, however, as such, backed up by negative situational sanctions; they are backed up, rather, by negative internal sanctions. (One should not say "merely" by negative internal sanctions, for these sanctions may be subjectively more painful than many negative situational sanctions.) Norms, on the other hand, are more often backed up by negative situational sanctions as well as by contingent internal and external (attitudinal) disapproval. This is one distinction, though not an absolute one. A second distinction is that norms in content are more specifically related to the situation of action and in this sense give more specific normative direction. An example of a "value" in Parsons's sense is "equality before the law." This does not tell anyone specifically what to do, although we might be able to recognize specific violations of it.

In Parsonian theory (which is by far the most highly developed form of "structural-functional" theory), values are related to norms in at least two important ways. First, values "legitimate" norms (or, of course, make norms "illegitimate" if the norms are inconsistent with the values). Second, values are a source of norms in the sense that they provide standards for the formation of new norms.

It seems to me that Petrazycki has some ideas not altogether different from these, especially if we take into account his discussion as well as his formal definitions. For him, "morality" is often a source of "law." We have seen that, at times, he uses "intuitive law" in a sense fairly close to "values," and that "positive law" (close at times to formal norms with negative situational sanctions) is in trouble if it is out of harmony with "intuitive law" ("values"). At any rate, I suggest that this comparison may sharpen up Petrazycki's ideas and make them more useful.

Petrazycki as a Structural-Functional Theorist

It is my contention that at least implicitly Petrazycki was a structural-functional theorist. The chief difficulty is that he was rather uncomfortable with the concept of legal norm, but I shall argue that his analysis of legal impulsions and in particular his analysis of official positive law strongly imply that he regarded as very important the sort of thing structural-functional theorists mean by social structure. As for the "functional" part, here there is no difficulty, for Petrazycki explicitly thought and wrote in functional terms.

In modern structural-functional theory, the structure of social systems is normative and cultural. It is the basis of legitimate expectations in social interaction, expectations that on the whole (but to varying extents) are fulfilled because the normative elements are internalized in many personalities, are the basis for the structuring and security of many interests, and are backed up by sanctions. Deviant behavior does occur, but it is called "deviant" because of the existence of a normative standard of some kind; and the regulating or controlling aspect of social structure includes the fact that various people, who might be called formal and informal agents of social control, seek to discourage others from following the deviant's example. Social "control" also includes the operation of guides and checks internal to the personality and not necessarily requiring, in particular situations, any agency of control external to the self. This self-control is "social" to the extent that the inner guides and checks are due to the internalization of social-structural values and norms.

Like any other scientific model, the one we have briefly described is not intended to be a description of concrete reality. Along with other features not treated here, it is a tool for the analysis of very important aspects of social process, for example, the production of goods and services and the "production" of solidarity. The model in no way conceives of action as mechanical—for example, as determined by conditioned reflexes or by a normative order. There are rules, some of them legal, for the creation and use of money, for example, and these rules are empirically of great importance for understanding not only the functioning of the economy but also its relations with the other functional subsystems of society. Nevertheless, these rules do not determine the specific content of transactions involving money; therefore they do not determine, although they profoundly affect, the aggregate functions of these transactions.

Petrazycki doubted the "reality" of norms. He calls them "projections" of some kind. This language seems to have something to do with confining the word reality to physical objects. Anyone may do this, of course, but I see little point in it. In any case, this usage of words does not affect the scientific substance of Petrazycki's work. He rightly regards as important the tendencies toward uniformity, consistency, and universalism in the legal system; and he analyzes some of the important bases of these tendencies. If we ask in what aspects of diverse legal impulsions of many different people there could be tendencies toward uniformity, consistency, and universalism, I doubt if the correct or pertinent answer is that a certain amount of adrenalin (epinephrine) is involved in all these impulsions. It is more pertinent that in these legal impulsions there are tendencies to uniformity, consistency, and universalism in the content of the felt obligations and rights that are involved —that is to say, in the legal norms. To be sure, these norms are nonphysical abstractions from the legal impulsions, but I do not see that their abstractness makes them any less "real" than adrenalin. Whenever we talk about anything (legal norms, adrenalin, or for that matter, legal impulsions) we are not talking about concrete reality but about some aspects of it.

We have to conclude, I think, that legal norms are extremely important in Petrazycki's thinking, and so are the social-structural aspects of some of these norms. Highly relevant here is the excellent discussion by Alexander Peczenik in the present volume.

Petrazycki's analysis of the law is also in functional terms. The summary of this aspect of his work that is contained in Lande's paper in the present volume accurately reflects, I think, the much longer treatment by Petrazycki himself in *Law and Morality*.

The most important systematic treatment of the concept of function in modern structural-functional theory is to be found in the works of Talcott Parsons. I am going to describe this scheme very briefly as a kind of background for making a few points about the functional aspect of Petrazycki's work. Parsons distinguishes four types of functions.[3] His scheme arises from two basic distinctions: first, the distinction between internal and external problems of the system; second, the distinction between instrumentality and consummation. The result of cross-classification is the conception that every type of "action" system, including systems of social interaction, has four functional subsystems, one for each of the problems (or categories of problems).

The economy is the external-instrumental functional subsystem of a "society" (a comprehensive type of social system). It produces generalized means for processes of goal attainment. In this scheme, the "polity" is the external-consummatory functional subsystem of a "society." It is concerned with the complex processes of goal attainment themselves.

The "internal" functional subsystems have to do with the subjective orientation of the units in the system. The "units" of a social system are subcollectivities and social roles. The internal-consummatory functional subsystem of a society has to do with the interrelations of units, in particular with the reduction of conflict and the (more or less successful) production of solidarity (hence the integrative subsystem of a society is called the societal community). Fundamental to it are "norms," legal and nonlegal.

The internal-instrumental functional subsystem of a society "maintains" the continuity of the values and value commitments of the constituent units. The terms "maintain" and "maintenance," however, do not imply absence of change; they do imply relative stability through time. The sense in which the subsystem for the "maintenance" of values is "instrumental" may not be immediately obvious. From the point of view of units themselves (the "subjective" point of view), maintenance of societal values (through socialization and other processes, for example, participation in ritual) is not at all likely to be regarded as "instrumental" (a means for something else). On the contrary, maintenance of societal values, insofar as it is a conscious process, is likely to be regarded as an end in itself. From the functional point of view, however (that is, from the point of view of the observer-theorist, the "objective" point of view, or, rather, one of many possible objective points of view), commitment to values *is* a kind of resource or generalized means. It is in this sense "instrumental" for the system as a whole but in particular for the internal-consummatory subsystem (the societal community or integrative system). This appears above all in three contexts: (a) A fundamental "instrumental" input to the process of creating and re-creating solidarity (in the integrative system) is commitment to common or shared values; (b) When norms (in the integrative system) are called into question, they have to be legitimated in terms of values (to which units are committed); (c) Furthermore, when norms become unsatisfactory and a search is made for new ones, the social *values* give direction to the search and eventually legitimation to the new norms. Thus the functional subsystem for "maintaining" values is a source of "stable" direction and legitimation to the whole social system. In a violent social revolution, of course, a new "cybernetic" hierarchy of control is set up, with new values (to some extent) at the top. But violent social revolutions in this sense do not occur every day.

There is a temporal aspect to the difference between "instrumental" and "consummatory" subsystems. In pursuing goals, one first gathers means and then combines them; and even in choosing goals one first considers, among other things, the means that are available or can be made available. These temporal aspects are involved in the relations between the economy and the polity (respectively, the instrumental and consummatory external subsystems of a society). So with the subsystem for the maintenance of values and the integrative subsystem, to which norms are central (respectively, the instrumental and consummatory internal subsystems of a society), it is in part the commitment to certain values that leads to the desire and will to join and support some organizations rather than others; and, on the part of members of an organization, the more or less common prior commitment to the same values is a more or less stable basis of its continued solidarity.

Clear awareness of system, functions, structure, and processes is no more to be expected of the participants in a social system than we expect a knowledge of linguistics or, indeed, technical knowledge even of their native language on the part of average speakers. The "subjective" point of view is essential in some of the data to be gathered, but it is not enough. What data to gather, and how to interpret their significance for the system, can only be decided on the basis of an "objective" conceptual scheme.

The main point to make about Petrazycki's treatment of function is that his "concrete" discussion is better than his formal analytical scheme. He discusses contract and property and authority. Concretely he was certainly aware of the fact that families and churches, for example, tend to inculcate and renew value commitments in the sense of the discussion above, and he was of course well aware of the fact that the law is highly relevant in and to families and churches. He was certainly aware of the fact that courts settle disputes and thus have an integrative function, and of the fact that the functioning of the courts is also subject to law. Yet Lande's summary is accurate as far as Petrazycki's formal analytical scheme is concerned: "Petrazycki discerns two different social functions of law: the distributive, controlling the distribution and the circulation of goods, and the organizational, establishing the structure of groups. The first produces the economic system; the second, the political system, especially the state."[4] In light of more recent thinking, these statements are not wrong; but I think it is obvious that they do not make enough distinctions. On the other hand, it was no small merit in Petrazycki's work that he regarded the concept of function as theoretically important. It should be pointed out, also, that this concept logically implies the concept of an empirical *system* of some kind, a system for which something is said to be functional. Not all social scientists of Petrazycki's time or since have gone as far as he did in seeing the importance of social system and of functional reference points for the analysis of structure and process.

The Educational Function of the Law

What Petrazycki called the educational function of the law is treated in modern structural-functional theory also, but of course in somewhat different terms. I think that readers of Petrazycki might be interested in how Parsons would phrase the sort of thing Petrazycki was talking about.

Parsons treats the functioning of a society as a complex set of processes in which four values are implemented, one for each of the fundamental functional subsystems. For example, the value principle of the economy is utility. Further, involved in the processes of value implementation are four generalized symbolic media, one anchored in each of the functional subsystems. For example, the generalized symbolic medium anchored in the economy is money. Furthermore, each of the generalized symbolic media stands for or symbolizes the value of the functional subsystem in which it is anchored. For example, money symbolizes utility. Still further, each of the generalized symbolic media also stands for one of the four types of sanctions. For example, money stands for positive situational sanctions.

Money is said to symbolize utility and a whole category of transactions in which utility is involved, first, because money commands the factors of production (of utility) and, second, because it can be exchanged for goods and services that "have" utility (that is, result from the implementation of the value principle of utility). Similarly, Parsons treats "influence" as a generalized symbolic medium, only in this case it symbolizes the value principle of the integrative system, namely solidarity. Influence "buys" the factors for the production of solidarity, that is, for the implementation of this value principle. Influence can also be exchanged for intrinsic solidarity, that is, for the result of implementing the value principle of solidarity.

What does a unit's influence depend upon? Ultimately it depends upon two things, first, the presumption that the unit has loyalty to "the group" and participates in the solidarity of the group, and second, the presumption that the unit, in attempting to persuade, that is, in using influence, is in a position to know what it is advising, has some skill in a special field of knowledge and a category of situations. The prestige of the unit—the basis of its influence—rests on some sort of aggregate of judgments concerning these two matters. Parsons goes into this in some detail.

Now take the law, in the sense in which "law" involves lawyers and clients, courts and conflicts of interest, and legislatures.Clients must be able to trust the lawyer's loyalty and competence. That is, the lawyer uses influence. He is presumed to be an expert in "the law," a highly complex field; and he is "committed" to defending his clients while maintaining the pattern integrity of the law. The judges in courts of law have a certain amount of prestige, which gives their decisions the capacity, to some extent, to reconcile not only winners but also losers, to each other and to the specific implications of the law for their cases. The judges' "opinions" have influence. So with legislatures: their members, through their influence, were able to get themselves elected to improve the public welfare, and now their collective decisions, presumably taken within the framework of the Constitution and with legal counsel, have a great deal of influence also, with the result that many people now have "legal impulsions" they would otherwise not have. Moreover, through the operation of influence these legal impulsions acquire and maintain a certain degree of uniformity in the sense that people agree to some extent about the meaning of the legal norms for a variety of situations. A cultural system is now part of the very structure of society, helping to control its further processes of value implementation. This total conception, provided it is not reified or treated in some essentialistic way, is obviously far more helpful, as a tool for analyzing society, than the conception of a series of unique encounters and exchanges. It is an indication of its merit that it is able to incorporate, in more generalized form, one of Petrazycki's most fundamental empirical insights. Incidentally, one of the most basic aspects of the normative order of any society, including the legal order, is that it regulates the creation and "spending" of all four of the generalized symbolic media.

Petrazycki on Sociocultural Evolution

Since Lande's paper is printed in this volume, I can summarize Petrazycki's evolutionary theory very briefly here. He thought that social evolution involves three tendencies, which he called "the tendency of increased demands," "the tendency to change incentives" (toward "higher" and more effective incentives for people in their performance of socially important tasks), and "the tendency to diminish motivational pressure" (specifically, the tendency toward *lesser* rewards but also less severe punishments).

He thought that social evolution in the form of these three tendencies is present in every social system; but he emphasized that these are tendencies only, that they are sometimes or always counteracted to some extent, and that retrogression ("retrogressive evolution") does occur sometimes. (On the whole, however, the term "social evolution" refers to social "progress.") Thus, in one respect, Petrazycki was a nineteenth-century evolutionary thinker and in another respect was unlike at least some nineteenth-century evolutionary thinkers, notably Marx. He was in the nineteenth-century tradition in that he thought of social evolution as something operating in every social system. He was unlike Marx in that he did not think of evolutionary tendencies as being inevitably successful. (It is not clear, to me, whether or not Petrazycki thought that every society, to the extent to which evolutionary processes are successful in it, must go through "stages" of evolution in the same sequence.[5])

Petrazycki also deals with the *processes* of social evolution. As far as I have been able to understand his thought, we can distinguish at least six of these processes:

(1) The first is the most vague; and in a sense we might regard the second and the third, and perhaps the others, as a "spelling out" of the first. At any rate, Petrazycki postulated an inherent teleology, an unconscious selective process in social evolution, a "puzzling purposefulness" (Lande). The ultimate end of this process is something like the brotherhood of man, a human brotherhood of mutual love and benevolence. (I think it is reasonably clear that the source of this conception, for Petrazycki, was Christianity.)

(2) The second process (or an aspect of the first) is "impulsive induction," a process essentially like unconscious conditioning by the reenforcement of "beneficial" "impulsions" and the gradual elimination of those that are "harmful." Lande characterizes it as follows: "The theory assumes that the animal psyche has a tendency to react with repellent impulses to an event which brings pain and annoyance, and with attractive impulses to an event which brings pleasure. The further experience results in reinforcement of the relevant associations, and in a decline of the accidental ones."[6]

In human beings, reason helps in the process of "natural selection" of impulsions favorable to the social system.

There is a latent competition going on in a society, something like a Darwinian struggle for survival, only in "the social process" it is not so much a struggle "to the death" of people or groups as it is a "natural selection" of ideas and even "impulsions."

(3) Through cultural diffusion, the field of operation of this selective process is widened, so that even better ideas and impulsions can be selected out.

(4) Eventually (rather soon) "official positive law," by which Petrazycki means what most people call simply "law," develops. The formal machinery of legislatures, courts, and enforcement agencies has a tendency to unify varying legal impulsions.

(5) The science of jurisprudence develops and carries the same tendency further. In addition, jurisprudence has a tendency to make social-structural law more universalistic.[7]

(6) Finally, a science of law of a different kind also develops, what we might call a sociology of law, on the basis of which a kind of legal engineering can be developed. In this way the process of social evolution can be rationally controlled and perhaps speeded up.

The most interesting part of this evolutionary theory, to me, is the three tendencies, which I have not described in detail because they are discussed in Lande's paper (where, in fact, I learned about them). These tendencies are treated in a different way in the most elaborate contemporary structural-functional theory of sociocultural evolution, that of Talcott Parsons. Rather than focusing upon these resemblances, however, I think it more useful to discuss certain differences between Petrazycki and Parsons. Space does not permit any attempt on my part to give Parsons's complete theory, which is rather complex.

(1) Whereas I think Petrazycki emphasized love in the Christian sense of *agape* as the end, and partly as the process itself, of social evolution, Parsons stresses "enhanced adaptive capacity"—not only adaptation, note, but enhanced adaptive capacity, a gradual development of flexibility, such that more advanced societies can handle a greater range of environmental exigencies and have greater and greater control *over* their environment. This enhanced adaptive capacity, moreover, is not the direct result of larger size of the population, for example; it is a result of cultural and sociocultural change. It is characteristic of Petrazycki that he conceives of sociocultural evolution with a primarily "psychological" emphasis. For him, progress, one could say, is essentially the development in average persons of a greater sense of responsibility and greater benevolence.

It should be pointed out, however, that *agape* is by no means unconnected with enhanced adaptive capacity. Flexibility in the social system does indeed involve value commitments and a high average sense of responsibility, initiative, and judgment in "spending" these generalized commitments. Further, as we have already noted earlier, value commitments are an important resource for creating and re-creating solidarity (which is fairly close to the mutual concern that would be the practical expression of widespread "love" or benevolence). Finally, strength in the integrative system, which builds solidarity as measured by consensus at several levels, is a necessary foundation for effective and efficient collective goal-attainment and (economic) production of generalized facilities. Simply put, cooperation requires some degree of integration. We shall have a little more to say about "love" and benevolence below.

(2) It is also characteristic of Petrazycki's "psychological" bias that he conceives of the process of "natural selection" in sociocultural evolution essentially as the resultant of individual learning processes in which "re-enforcement" and association play a large part.

At first glance this is fairly plausible, and I think there is something to it even at second glance. However, sociocultural evolution is primarily an affair of social and cultural systems and only secondarily and derivatively a matter of individual learning. What has to be explained is not so much the psychological process of learning but social-system variation in the development of new things to learn. To be sure, individuals must be involved in cultural, including social-structural, innovation, but it is difficult to explain *variation* in rates of effective innovation by reference to something that is presumably roughly *constant* from one social system to another, namely the operation of the principles of re-enforcement.

What is needed is a distinction between socialization and institutionalization. Socialization is a learning process; it is the process by which children and other members or prospective members of a social system learn the culture, including the skills, necessary for knowledgeable and competent participation in the system. The process is, of course, successful to varying degrees. In this process the mechanisms that Petrazycki emphasizes are indeed very important. When fully socialized members act as socializing agents, they are able to reward responses selectively and create the proper associations. In other words, these mechanisms work reasonably well within a social structure that is already established. They are also presumably at work in the process of establishing social structure, but in general this process is different enough from socialization to warrant a somewhat special framework of analysis.

The term that Parsons and some others use for the complex process in which something new is established in the structure of a social system is institutionalization. As far as sociocultural evolution is concerned, Parsons has followed Spencer and Durkheim in recognizing that one of the general trends is toward more complex social structure. (Petrazycki also recognized this fact, but he does not make it central to his analysis, as Parsons does.) Further, in analyzing this complexity, Parsons keeps at least five points firmly in mind throughout: (a) The basic trend of sociocultural evolution is toward enhanced adaptive capacity *of the sociocultural system* (secondarily and derivatively of individuals); (b) The concept of functional problems is essential for the analysis of comparative social structure (including analysis of structural change)—social structure, hence a structural change, is significant to the social system in question because it guides or controls the action of constituent units in the implementation of certain values, hence in the "meeting" or "solution" of the functional problems. In an evolutionary perspective, "enhanced adaptive capacity" is a shorthand term for greater effectiveness in meeting any one or any combination of the functional problems; (c) The greater complexity of more "advanced" social systems is essentially greater differentiation in types of subcollectivity and social role, differentiation with respect to both structure and function; (d) The attempt to bring about greater differentiation often (perhaps usually) provokes some social opposition, and even if the differentiation does succeed it is likely to create new integrative problems for the social system. The whole process of institutionalization therefore must include an integrative phase or a succession of integrative phases; (e) For new social structure to be established in a social system, it is not enough that ideas be available or even that available ideas be functionally desirable for the system. The favorable reception of new "suggestions," so to speak (new structural "candidates" for inclusion in the social order), depends upon a certain favorableness in the existing sociocultural system. The other side of the coin is that some of the conditions necessary for successful institutionalization may be lacking.

The complete process of institutionalization can be broken down into four subsidiary processes. A process of (a) "differentiation" takes place in a collectivity or collectivities (in the goal-attainment system), in the sense that two functions once performed by a single unit or unit type come to be separated, so that each is now performed by a unit of more specialized type. As a result of this differentiation (b) "adaptive upgrading" occurs: that is, the functions, especially those performed by the new unit, get to be performed more effectively, and this fact is recognized outside the circle in which the innovation occurred. Nevertheless, "big" innovations also tend to arouse opposition. The repercussions of innovative change then cause a series of disturbances that require integrative changes (c), "inclusion," at the norm level. The new types of collective unit must be "included," as Parsons says—must become integrated aspects of a larger system. Adjustive changes must occur. Finally, the differentiation/integration process involves (d) "value generalization." This means that the value system is stretched, in the sense that its values now cover or can be seen to cover, among the more specific possibilities it can legitimate, the new norms, types of subcollectivity, and types of role. The whole process of differentiation/integration, to get off the ground at all, requires values generalized enough to permit the legitimizing of the structural changes. Nevertheless, we can also say that at the end of the whole process one of the results is value generalization in the sense that "everyone" now accepts the structural changes as legitimate. They have become institutionalized.[8]

Such an evolutionary sequence, resulting in enhanced adaptive capacity of the society, requires special conditions to get going and to be successful.[9] First, there must be "strain"—dissatisfaction with the level of functioning. Second, someone must be able to see some possible improvement. Third, there must be sufficiently generalized values to legitimize the proposed structural change (this may require, in some cases, the crystallization of a "revolutionary" "ideology"). Fourth, the proponents of change must be able to overcome or neutralize opposition. Fifth, for the change to be fully institutionalized, it is necessary for the interest structure and the allocation of rewards and punishments to become intermeshed with it. Four and five are part of the process of "inclusion."

The specifically integrative aspect or phase of evolution, which Parsons calls "inclusion," may involve bringing new or hitherto underprivileged segments of the population, say ethnic minorities, into the legal and realistic enjoyment of equal rights with the formerly dominant and privileged segments of the population. Among these rights, in modern times, are religious freedom, equality of opportunity for an education, equality before the law, equality of voting rights, equality of the right to hold public office, and equality of opportunity for employment in general.[10] In fact, Parsons sees in the present period of social evolution a growing tendency to regard all forms of inequality and constraint as illegitimate unless they can be justified in functional terms.[11] It seems to me that the broad equivalent, in Parsons, of Petrazycki's emphasis on the growth of "love" and benevolence is the concept of inclusion and the idea that increasingly constraints and inequalities must be justified in functional terms for the society as a whole, on the whole. Petrazycki's tendencies toward "increased demands," "change of incentives," and "diminished motivational pressure," which are accompanied by and partly consist in greater mutual concern, depend not only upon sufficiently generalized "religious" ideas and societal values but also upon lower-level social structure and especially upon rights. Solidarity involves, on the part of participants in a social system, not only a common concern for the general welfare but recognition of and concern for one another's legitimate self-interests.

I can perhaps drive home a basic point in the foregoing somewhat complex discussion by saying that whereas for Petrazycki the analog of "natural selection" (in biological evolution) is "impulsive induction," the selection of better adapted psychological impulsions (complexes of motivation), for Parsons the analog of "natural selection" is the process of "inclusion" (and rejection) of attempts to institutionalize social-structural innovations.

(3) For Parsons, a particularly important example of differentiation is the clear-cut differentiation between the social system and the cultural system; in this process the invention of writing played an important role. A social system, of course, is a system of social interaction. In its primary meaning, "culture" consists of symbols ("codes" and "messages," of which "law" is an important example) that arise gradually in the course of social interaction. But once it exists, "culture" regulates social interaction itself; in fact, for Parsons "action" in the technical sense involves culture by definition. In a slightly different sense, "culture" (now viewed as an "action" system) exists to the extent that interacting people are devoting their attention to the functional problems of systems of symbols, for example, to theology, to ethics, or to the theory or to the unsolved problems of a particular science.

Since culture first arises in social interaction and then comes to control or regulate it, obviously in the very early stages of sociocultural evolution the role of culture must have been very small. Even in "primitive" societies today, what culture there is is deeply and directly involved in the system of social interaction itself—in that sense, is "fused" with it. Only in more advanced societies is "culture" as a set of "action systems" more clearly differentiated, with of course very great accompanying enhancement of the adaptive capacity of society. Broadly speaking, there is an evolutionary tendency for culture (apart from language itself, the most important "code" for communication, the cultural result of a very long process of social interaction) to become at some point more self-consciously organized, until at last we find organizations, such as the modern university, that are social but also cultural in a special sense, being collectivities specifically set up and consciously organized to create and to transmit culture.

(4) With regard to levels of social structure, the evolutionary process is again from fusion to differentiation. As Durkheim pointed out, in primitive societies, that is, societies in the early stages of evolution, there is relatively little variation in beliefs and sentiments. The *conscience collective* is strict and rather detailed, but detailed in the same way (relatively speaking) for all; there is "mechanical" solidarity: this is virtually equivalent to saying that values and norms are "fused," so to speak; even the details of normatively prescribed behavior are sacred, theoretically not subject to change, stagnant. (In passing, Petrazycki makes a similar observation about "customary law," which of course, in his sense, was an early form of law;[12] but he does not seem to grasp fully the connection of this point with fusion and differentiation.) In later stages, values remain relatively stable and "sacred," but norms

(relatively specific prescriptions and proscriptions) cease to be sacred and hence are subject to change. After all, legislatures are in general expected to reconsider existing laws and enact new ones from time to time.

To say that detailed prescriptions cease to be sacred, while values tend to remain so, is equivalent to saying that values must become more general in character, and Durkheim recognized this. The universalistic rule of law as a *standard* is clearly a value, not a norm; but it comes late in the evolutionary process. "Equality of opportunity" is another example. In fact, implicit in every society (even in primitive societies) are four values, one for each of the functional problems; but it is only late in the evolutionary process that these values can be explicitly recognized in their most general form. Thus, we no longer implement the value of utility (the value for the economy) by merely following traditional ways; on the contrary, the value of utility, once it is clearly recognized, can flexibly legitimize a great many more specific norms and changes in norms.

(5) A point emphasized by Max Weber (and not always noticed even today in discussions of Weber) is that the conditions for successful original social-structural innovation are very different from the conditions for later adoption of innovations through diffusion. This point is beautifully developed by Parsons.[13]

Concluding Comments

It is interesting, I think, to compare Petrazycki with Durkheim and Weber, who were roughly his contemporaries. Despite a certain "psychologistic" bias (not strong enough, perhaps, to be called reductionism), Petrazycki did recognize the fact that *social* structure exists and has important consequences for motivation. Durkheim, despite his "sociologistic" bias, was well aware that religion and social structure exist in the personalities of individuals.[14] I think that Durkheim's theory of evolution was superior in some respects. He had a much more profound understanding of the role of religion in human societies. Appreciating the tremendous importance of the division of labor for evolution, he stressed the process of differentiation and integration. He called attention to the importance of the progressive differentiation of values and norms.

Max Weber did not use the structural-functional approach systematically, although he appreciated its value to some extent. He understood and demonstrated the importance of religious variation. He made great advances in the analysis of structural variation more generally. His analysis of the social and cultural results of the process of "rationalization" in the West, compared with the results of different processes of rationalization elsewhere, remains a fundamental reference point for the study of evolution.

It is a great pity that Petrazycki's sociological manuscripts, mentioned by Lande, were lost, and that the Russian Revolution prevented his work from having the influence it might have had, not only in Russia but in the world at large. His theory was clearly superior to that of Marx in some respects, though not in others. Like Max Weber, he clearly appreciated the tremendous importance of "law" and "morality" in human societies. He did not have any dogma about the inevitability of evolutionary stages or the decisive role of class conflict. Perhaps his most attractive idea was his conception that law can be used to help social progress. It is fitting, therefore, that the present volume should close with Jan Gorecki's careful treatment of Petrazycki's ideas about social engineering through law.

[1]Talcott Parsons, *Politics and Social Structure* (New York: The Free Press, 1969), p. 448.

[2]Petrazycki, *Law and Morality*, pp. 232-233.

[3]See especially "Some Problems of General Theory in Sociology," John C. McKinney and Edward A. Tiryakian, eds., *Theoretical Sociology. Perspectives and Developments* (New York: Appleton-Century-Crofts, 1970), pp. 28-36.

[4]Pages 26-27 of present volume.

[5]Because culture can be diffused, it is clearly not true that different societies go through the same sequence of stages to the extent to which the evolutionary process occurs in them. The so-called developing societies today are able to take advantage of evolutionary advances that arose first in the West and that, as Max Weber showed, could hardly have arisen on the sociocultural basis of the developing countries themselves. (See also Talcott Parsons, *Structure and Process in Modern Societies* [Glencoe, Ill.: The Free Press, 1960], Chap. 3; and "Christianity," David L. Sills, ed., *International Encyclopedia of the Social Sciences* [New York: Macmillan and The Free Press, 1968]). Weber's work helps us to understand why sociocultural evolution is not rectilinear. Not only may retrogression occur, but also some societies become relatively fixed in a particular sociocultural condition. In fact, even with increasing diffusion of culture in the foreseeable future, special "local" circumstances may make it possible for some societies to remain fairly "primitive," just as some "lower" species have been able to survive because they are well adapted to very stable specific environments.

[6]Page 33 of the present volume.

[7]See Petrazycki's remarkable statement in *Law and Morality*, pp. 144-145.

[8]Talcott Parsons, "Commentary on Clark," *Sociological Inquiry*, 42 (1972), 299-308.

[9]Besides Talcott Parsons, *Societies: Evolutionary and Comparative Perspectives* (Englewood Cliffs, N.J.: Prentice-Hall, 1966) and *The System of Modern Societies*

(Englewood Cliffs, N.J.: Prentice-Hall, 1971), see Neil J. Smelser, *Social Change in the Industrial Revolution. An Application of Theory to the British Cotton Industry* (Chicago: University of Chicago Press, 1959), and *Essays in Sociological Explanation* (Englewood Cliffs, N.J.: Prentice-Hall, 1968), pp. 251-254.

[10]Talcott Parsons, *Sociological Theory and Modern Society* (New York: The Free Press, 1967). See chapters entitled "Durkheim's Contribution to the Theory of Integration of Social Systems" (originally 1959), "Evolutionary Universals" (originally 1964), and "Full Citizenship for the Negro American?" (originally 1966).

[11]For Talcott Parsons's complex argument, which is organized in terms of the scheme of four functional subsystems, see "Equality and Inequality in Modern Society, or Social Stratification Revisited," *Sociological Inquiry*, 40 (1970), 13-72.

[12]Petrazycki, *Law and Morality*, p. 269.

[13]Parsons, *Structure and Process in Modern Societies*, chap. 3.

[14]I disagree with Lande's interpretation of Durkheim. Despite a common impression to the contrary, Durkheim did not have a "mystical" conception of society as existing independently of individuals. What Durkheim rightly emphasized is that, from the point of view of any given individual, social structure is both internal and external. It is "in" individuals, but it is also an important part of the *milieu social.*

CHAPTER

5

Interaction, Law, and Morality: The Contributions of Leon Petrazycki

NORMAN K. DENZIN

The sociological and social psychological formulations of Leon Petrazycki remain largely unknown and unattended to by twentieth-century American sociologists. With the exceptions of the writings of his former students, Sorokin,[1] Timasheff,[2] and Gurvitch,[3] it is impossible to find a reference to his work in any contemporary text on sociological theory, or in the more narrowly defined field of the sociology of law. As a consequence, the issues he addressed, most notably a sociological theory of law and morality, and a general sociology, remain unknown to the contemporary student of everyday social life. Yet, to a remarkable degree, his perspective anticipated and overlaps with the uniquely American school of thought known as pragmatism and symbolic interactionism.[4]

It is not my intention in this essay to offer a full-scale analysis of Petrazycki's theories of law and society.[5] My aims are narrower. I shall focus on the following elements of Petrazycki's work: (1) his concept of law and morality; (2) his treatment of the introspective method; (3) his analysis of motives, motivation, and his conception of thought, learning, and psychology; (4) his views of domestic life and intimate relationships and their legal foundations.

I shall review his underlying assumptions on these issues and compare and contrast them to the social psychology of symbolic interactionism. My intent is to draw scholars' attention to his work, in the hope that a more faithfully systematic view of law, morality, and interaction can be constructed.

The Theoretical and Methodological Assumptions of Symbolic Interactionism

It is necessary to begin with a brief discussion of symbolic interactionism, so as to better highlight Petrazycki's parallels with this school of thought. *Theoretically*, the symbolic interactionist assumes that social reality, as it is sensed, known, and scientifically studied, is a human construct. It is constructed, produced, and sustained by everyday actors, who in the course of taking their own and other's perspectives forge unique definitions of the situation. Reality, as such, consists of those social objects actors take seriously. Objects, which can be defined as anything the actor can separate from anything else and act toward in a unitary fashion, have meaning only insofar as actors act toward them. That is, the meaning of the object arises out of the behaviors directed toward it.[6] In this sense, meaning does not reside in objects; rather, it is conferred on objects during the course of interaction.

The interactionist views the human organism in active terms. The human is active from the moment of birth. Activity as such is a constant. Its organization is not. This proposition makes the question of motivation—that is, what propels the organism into action—irrelevant, for the organism is continuously active. What does become central, however, is the question of motives and accounts. What explanations does the actor offer for his or her behavior? (This question is central to Petrazycki's distinction between law and morality, and between purposive, normative, and fundamental actions, which will be elaborated below.)

The interactionist further assumes that the organism enters the world neurologically neutral. Drives, wishes, impulsions, or emotions are absent from its behavioral repertoires. It becomes what it becomes by virtue of social experience. Its activity is not a response to unmediated neurological or physiological drives. The human, then, actively engages in minded, symbolic behavior. He is capable of taking his own and other's perspectives in concrete interactional settings. Human activity is differentially self-reflexive. Self-reflexive behavior arises in those situations where custom, ritual, law, and morality become problematic. Problematic, or blocked, acts produce self-conscious behavior. In the course of taking their own perspective, actors find that they must take account of other objects, or of other actors. Interaction emerges from such episodes, and can be defined as those instances when two or more individuals fit their respective lines of action into a joint, focused performance. Interaction is symbolic quite simply because it involves individuals placing themselves in one another's perspective. Interaction is negotiated and emergent—that is, this fitting together process can never be fully predicted or anticipated by each actor. It takes on an emergent tone as each individual judges and responds to the actions and utterances of the other individuals in the situation.

Methodologically, symbolic interactionism directs the investigator to take, to the best of his or her abilities, the perspectives of those studied.[7] It argues that the researcher must directly enter into the worlds of native people so as to construct a theory of their behavior that weds their attitudes with their action.[8] It demands that the investigator situate his observations in the routine worlds of the native actor. It suggests that sterile research techniques such as the laboratory experiment, the fixed-choice questionnaire, or the elaborate mathematical model are of little use until they have been grounded in the experiences and thoughts of the native.[9]

If reality is socially constructed and constantly shifting, then it can be argued that, at best, the sociologist can only hope for successfully better approximations of that reality he has under inspection. No method or theory will ever catch all of the subtle features of a socially produced social world. As a consequence, the interactionist employs the method of triangulation. He will use any and all methodologies that yield some knowledge about the processes being studied. Central to his methodological stance will be a combined use of participant observation, life history construction, and introspection. The interactionist takes himself seriously, and argues that his own thoughts and actions are valid sources of data on everyday social life.[10]

In assembling his observations into a theoretically coherent causal model, the interactionist attempts to forge sequential-phaselike propositional networks. He attempts to uncover the underlying processes that produce the phenomenon in question, and assumes that no event is the product of one sufficient condition. He seeks the necessary conditions that, when combined, shape the behaviors he is studying. Simplistic bivariate, independent-dependent causal models are rejected for a more qualitative, sequential analysis in which variables become processes which, at alternative points in their causal career, can assume both independent and dependent causal status.

Summary of Interactionism

These few remarks establish the essential features of symbolic interactionism as a distinct approach to the study of human group life.

Human behavior is minded and symbolically self-reflexive in nature. Societies as complex interactive concerns are resolved into the interlaced patterns of interaction that both separate and join individuals into shifting webs of affiliation.[11] Reality is socially constructed by interacting individuals. Methodologically, the interactionist weds this constructionist view of reality with research activities that take him directly into the worlds of native actors.

The Theory and Methods of Leon Petrazycki: Parallels with Interactionism

The above discussion should immediately establish the parallels between Petrazycki's work and the essential thrust of symbolic interactionism. The following compatibilities in perspective can be noted. Like the interactionist, Petrazycki[12] held that the meanings of objects reside in action, actors, and thought. Consider the following remarks: "we must avoid the error of accepting as real that which seems to exist in a world external to the person experiencing such processes, and keep in mind that the corresponding real phenomena are to be found in the mind—and only in the mind—of that person."[13]

He carried this perspective one step further in his definition of law and legal behavior. "Legal phenomena consist of unique psychic processes . . . expressed, incidentally, in the unique form of ascribing to different beings (not only to people, but to beings of various other classes conceived in the mind), or to certain classes of such beings, 'duties' and 'rights'; so that these beings, so conceived of, are seemingly found in certain peculiar conditions of being bound or of possessing special objects ('rights'), and the like."[14] Petrazycki's devastating critique of the traditional jurisprudence is contained in the following passage: "The content of traditional legal science is tantamount to an optical illusion: it does not see legal phenomena where they actually occur, but discerns them where there is absolutely naught of them—where they cannot be found, observed, or known—that is to say, in a world external to the subject who is experiencing the legal phenomena."[15]

Law, for Petrazycki, was to be treated as a subjectively perceived phenomenon. Law exists as a social object in the everyday actions of actors. Its meaning lies in the behaviors such individuals bring to it. (This point will be elaborated below. It is necessary to note here that Petrazycki, like his revisionist Timasheff, noted several varieties of law: intuitive, domestic, statute, customary, book, official, and unofficial.)

Law does not reside in a social structure that is independent of the actions of individuals.

George Herbert Mead, who developed the foundations of symbolic interactionism,[16] treated the law and legal behavior in a fashion quite close to Petrazycki.

> In his acceptance of the law and dependency upon it the individual is at one with the community, while this very attitude carries with it the recognition of his responsibility to obey and support the law in its enforcement. So conceived the common law is an affirmation of citizenship. It is, however, a grave mistake to assume that the law itself and men's attitudes toward it can exist *in abstracto*. . . . It is not only a mistake, it is also a fundamental error, for all emotional attitudes—and even respect for law and a sense of responsibility are emotional attitudes—arise in response to concrete impulses.[17]

In this passage, Mead parallels Petrazycki's distinction between law and morality: law establishes a reciprocally binding relationship between actors. It sets up a set of rights and expectations. Morality, on the other hand, establishes obligations in the absence of rights.

Petrazycki's phenomenological view of reality led him to develop the following view of thought and action:

> our inward, psychic acts—such as anger or joy—cause various movements of the body which may be observed externally, and this is particularly so as to the bodily movements we produce in order to communicate to others some psychic condition or process (gesticulation, or the pronouncing and writing of words, and so forth). When we observe the same actions on the part of others, we can by analogy suppose—with more or less probability—that they are based on the same psychic experiences.[18]

In this passage he is suggesting that thoughts or attitudes provoke overt physical activity. The actor, he seems to suggest, enters into the process of organizing his own activity. (Later this point will be revised.) Compare, then, Petrazycki with Mead:

> Social psychology is behavioristic in the sense of starting off with observable activity—the dynamic, on-going social process, and the social acts which are its component elements—to be studied and analyzed scientifically. But it is not behavioristic in the sense of ignoring the inner experience of the individual—the inner phase of that process or activity. On the contrary, it is particularly concerned with the rise of such experience within the process as a whole. It simply works from the outside to the inside instead of from the inside to the outside, so to speak, in its endeavor to determine how such experience does arise within the proc-

ess. The act, then, not the tract, is the fundamental datum in both social and individual psychology when behavioristically conceived, and it has both an inner and an outer phase, an internal and an external phase.

These general remarks have to do with our point of appoach. It is behavioristic, but unlike Watsonian behaviorism it recognizes the parts of the act which do not come to external observation, and it emphasizes the act of the human individual in its natural social situation.[19]

Like Mead and the other symbolic interactionists,[20] Petrazycki argues that internal psychic acts and activities must be taken into account if a viable social psychology of human behavior is to be developed. (However, he departs from an interactionist view of the act when he attempts to classify internal impulsions, or "need-drive" states, which move the human in one direction as opposed to another. This feature of his work will be discussed below under the question of his treatment of motives and motivation. At this juncture, it is sufficient to note that his social psychology emphasized internal, covert acts as central data for sociology.)

Methodologically, Petrazycki argues that introspection was the only proper method of observing legal phenomena. Like the interactionist, his view of objects and action led him to the conclusion that the researcher must actively enter the worlds of everyday actors if his theory of law and morality was to be grounded in the experiences of those individuals. He argues:

The proper, and the only possible, method of observing legal phenomena must, therefore, be the method of self-observation: the introspective method.[21]

He defined the introspective method as: "(a) the directing of inward attention to the psychic phenomenon to be studied during the time when it is being experienced—self-observation in the narrow sense, such as the observation of hunger, thirst, or toothache, and the like—and (b) the inward observation of ideas—of 'images'—of previously experienced acts of a given class (such as recollections of last night's toothache)."[22] Two forms of introspection were delineated, simple and experimental: "Every sort of observation, including introspective observation, may be either simple or experimental. The experimental method means observation complicated by designedly influencing the phenomena to be observed—that is to say, by applying special means to evoke, to change, or to terminate them. If this is done relative to phenomena which are to be observed inwardly, this is the introspetive-experimental method."[23]

The bulk of Petrazycki's observation on law and morality rested on the introspective-experimental method. Introspection, as indicated above, is a central methodology of the interactionist. Blumer described Mead's strategies of observing social interaction as follows:

> how is human action constructed [?] Mead worked out his answer [to this question] . . . not by postulating an ideal society, but by close and persistent observation of those around him or himself. Where is there a more directly presented and ever accessible area of empirical happening for inquiry into the nature of human communication than the daily conversations one has with one's fellows? Where does one have a richer body of recurring instances of human beings fitting their lines of action to one another than that which takes place under one's nose? . . . The natural happenings which set the cardinal problems of human action occur continuously in the area of immediate experience and observation. It was such happenings that constructed the empirical matters that Mead studied with care, with persistence, and with his unusual gifts of originality.[24]

Petrazycki's contribution was to distinguish simple from experimental introspection. His method provides the scientist with a strategy for delineating the unique features of any class of social phenomena. His method is remarkably close to the use of *Verstehen*, as advocated by Weber:

> Understanding may be of two kinds: the first is direct observational understanding of the subjective meaning of a given act as such, including verbal utterances. We thus understand by direct observation, in this sense, the meaning of the proposition 2 X 2 = 4 when we hear or read it. This is a case of direct rational understanding of ideas. We also understand an outbreak of anger as manifested by facial expression, exclamations or irrational movements. This is direct observational understanding of irrational emotional reactions. . . .
>
> Understanding may, however, be of another sort, namely explanatory understanding. Thus we understand in terms of *motive* the meaning an actor attaches to the proposition twice two equals four, when he states it or writes it down, in that we understand what makes him do this at precisely this moment and in these circumstances. . . . Thus for a science which is concerned with the subjective meaning of action, explanation requires a grasp of the complex of meaning in which an actual course of understandable action thus interpreted belongs.[25]

Summary of Petrazycki and Interactionism

Leon Petrazycki's work, I have suggested, overlaps or parallels the underlying notions of symbolic interactionism in at least three crucial areas: his psychological view of objects, the law, and the methodology of the social sciences. His treatment of introspection, conceptually at least, moves beyond Mead and Cooley and converges with Weber's two conceptions of scientific understanding: direct observational and explanatory understanding. In these senses, Petrazycki should be judged as a heretofore unrecognized contributor to the pragmatist-interactionist school of thought. However, his perspective departs from interactionism in two crucially important ways. I turn next to those departures, which are embodied in his theory of action.

Petrazycki's Theory of Action: His View of Learning and the Impulsions

Petrazycki rejected the contemporary psychology of his time and developed a model of learning that was quite close to the research of Pavlov. (Neither Pavlov nor Petrazycki make reference to the other's work. There may have been a cross-fertilization of ideas, produced more by the climate of opinion operative during this period than by any direct contact between scientists. In any case, Petrazycki's view of impulsions is quite close to Pavlov's stimulus-response theory. For an early and still classic critique of Pavlov, see Mead.)[26]

Petrazycki argued that the conventional three-fold division of psychic behavior (which goes back at least to Plato) into cognitions, feelings, and active experiences was unsatisfactory. This was because the scheme ignored the relationship (bilateral or unilateral) between psychic states and actors. He offered the following division of psychic activity: "(1) bilateral, passive-active experiences (impulsions) and (2) unilateral experiences, falling into (a) unilateral-passive (cognitive and feeling) experiences, and (b) unilateral-active (will) experiences."[27] His rejection of the more general model rested on the following argument: "Cognitive experiences (of sight, hearing, taste, smell, touch, temperature and other sensations) and corresponding ideas and perceptions possess a unilateral-passive nature in the general sense: they are passive (*pati*) experiences. Feelings in the technical sense (pleasures and sufferings) likewise possess a unilateral-passive nature: they are passive experiences of the pleasant and the unpleasant. Will experiences—such as the will to continue to work regardless of fatigue—are unilateral-active experiences."[28]

He contended that another class of psychic activity could be isolated through self-observation: "Proper self-observation can reveal the existence of experiences in our psychic life not fitting within any one of the three categories, but possessing a bilateral, passive-active nature—containing passive experiences which are distinct from those of cognition and of feeling, as well as specific experiences (appetences)."[29] Having isolated this class of mental phenomena, he proceeded to argue that experiences of hunger, sex, and thirst were passive-active, bilateral experiences. He then offered a definition of impulsion:

> *We unite into a special class all the phenomena of the human and animal mind which possess this bilateral passive-active nature and term them impulsions.*[30]

Petrazycki's theory of learning and action rested on the discovery of these bilateral (passive-active) impulsions. This provided him with his theory of motives and motivation. He saw impulsions as performing the following functions for the organism:

> Impulsions perform the function of stimulating external movements of the body and other actions—such as intellectual work and other inward actions—and evoke directly the appropriate physiological and psychic processes. . . . Every day we experience many thousands of them. They govern our body and our mind. They evoke bodily movements which we make, the thoughts and the decisions which appear in our consciousness, and various other physical and psychic processes. Ruling our psychic life, these factors themselves remain, with rare exceptions, unnoted, and we are conscious only of deviations from their normal course: when either the waves of impulsions run extraordinarily high or they sink extraordinarily low; in the latter case, the peculiar, oppressive condition of boredom or apathy is noted.[31]

In this passage, Petrazycki comes dangerously close to arguing that the impulsion evokes its own response, independent of the definitions of the actor. In this sense his model approaches the classic stimulus-response paradigm of Pavlov, which argued that stimuli, or impulses, pass through the organism in such a way as to call out responses, independent of how the organism would define those stimuli. Thus, while Petrazycki could argue that objects carry no intrinsic meaning, when he began to formulate his theory of action he suspended his earlier constructionist (psychological) position in favor of a traditional jurisprudence causal model of social facts.

Consider the following quotations:

> Certain impulsions tend to evoke definite and specific conduct especially associated with them by nature; and since we term the systems of body

> movement and other physiological and psychological processes evoked by impulsions the responses thereto. . . . Thus hunger-appetite has its own definite and specifically characteristic response. . . . In precisely the same way there are special responses characteristic of thirst, sex excitation, curiosity, fear, shame, and countless other impulsions. . . . As a general formula defining the operation of impulsion with special responses (succinctly termed special impulsions) the following proposition may be established: special impulsions tend to turn the organism—the individual psycho-physical apparatus suited, in general, to the production of many and extremely diverse actions—into an apparatus especially adapted for the time being to the fulfillment of a definite biological function. . . .[32]

The stimulus evokes its own response. Sensing that this formulation approached tautology, Petrazycki offered the following disclaimer: "This formula does not purport to assert either that the responses to special impulsions are absolutely predetermined and uniform like the movements of machines, or that the same identical movements are repeated without change whenever a certain special impulsion is present. The predetermination of responses to special impulsions is relative, not absolute."[33]

Variations in response, he argued, are in part contingent on the character of the object being acted on—for example, different foods evoke different hunger and consumption patterns. Further, he suggested that lower animals were more likely to be fixed in their responses to various stimuli, while humans would be more variable. (In this sense he was moving beyond a strict Pavlov stimulus-response theory of human activity.) He states: "In men, certain impulsions are of so free and changeable a character that their predetermination is limited to the general direction of conduct. This is especially so as to the elements of man's mind which are most important from the point of view of social life, such as the impulsions whose responses consist of benevolent conduct toward others."[34] He cites love, ambition, vanity, malice, and hatred as instances of such impulsions. These impulsions he termed abstract or blanket. They serve "as stimuli to any conduct whatever: they incite specifically those responses whose ideas are experienced in association with them."[35]

We move now to the final argument in his theoretical structure: in large part everyday social life is made up of responses to these blanket impulsions. Law and morality belong to this impulsion class. He summarizes: "The stimuli of our behavior are, in general, either special impulsions (in which case, our conduct has the character of the specific action historically associated with the given impulsion), or blanket (abstract) impulsions (in which case the content of the idea of the conduct associated with the impulsion—of the action idea—defines the character and direction of our conduct)."[36]

Two broad classes of impulsions drive or motivate human activity: those which evoke specific responses, and those which evoke vague, actor-setting-object specific activities.

Petrazycki recognized a methodological problem with his formulations. If the impulsions go unnoticed, how can they be scientifically studied? The method of counteraction or the experimental method of diagnostics, which he more generally termed the method of provocation, was his answer, that is, deprive the organism of food to see how it responds to the hunger drive. Obstruct its activity and observe its response patterns. (This, of course, was Pavlov's strategy. Exactly how this method worked in the study of law and morality was elaborated in the *Theory of Law and State*.[37])

Problems with Petrazycki's Theory of Action

Disclaimers aside, Petrazycki has formulated a drive-reductionistic, static model of human activity. The organism is not continuously active, as an interactionist would argue. Rather, its behavior is a function of the impulsions it comes in contact with. When the stimulus object of an impulsion is located and acted on (responded to), the organism moves from a state of disequilibrium to one of stasis, or balance. The organism, then, is excited by external and internal stimuli, and these stimuli move through the organism in a subjectively neutral fashion. Petrazycki offers no way for the actor to actively define the meaning of any given impulsion. He offers no theory of minded, symbolic, self-reflexive behavior. Thus, while his view of objects and the law is phenomenological, his view of minded, mental behavior is reductionistic, and in essence denies the constructionist basis of his earlier formulation. Furthermore, the methods of introspection and provocation are not systematically developed in his own analysis. Consequently, his introspectionism could lead him close to a position of reification and psychological (and ultimately physiological) reductionism. (This problem is not unique to Petrazycki. A recent example can be found in Homans,[38] who, in an attempt to bring man back into contemporary sociology, found himself in the position of equating human behavior with the "pecking" patterns of pigeons.)

Law, Morality, and Interaction: Petrazycki Reconsidered

These criticisms aside, the more relevant question asks: "What do we learn about law, morality and everyday interaction from the formulations of Leon Petrazycki?" The answer is a great deal, and I next consider what I regard as his major contributions to the study of focused, face-to-face interaction.

Everyday life, for Petrazycki, was regarded as a rule-governed concern. Actors continually bring into play specifications or recipes for action. Petrazycki's analysis led to an isolation of two broad rule-related categories: law and morality. Each was regarded as a variant on ethical norms, or imperatives. He defined morality as those norms that "establish obligations free in respect to others: these authoritatively prescribe certain conduct for us but give others no claim or rights of any kind to fulfillment by us."[39] Legal norms, on the other hand, are seen as "establishing obligations for some—make these obligations secure in behalf of others: give the latter rights—claims—so that, in accordance with these norms, that to which some are bound is due to others as something authoritatively granted to them and made secure in their behalf: these are binding-exigent, imperative-attributive norms."[40] Morality, then, describes these recipes for action which are unilateral. They establish obligations, but not rights. Law ties actors into a reciprocated system of obligations and rights. It links them into an interconnected set of expectations, and in this sense Petrazycki was suggesting that law works to establish binding status-role relationships.[41]

Given these considerations, Petrazycki was led to the inevitable conclusion that law and morality could not be divorced from the everyday actions of individuals. That is, everyday life was to be viewed as a morally laden concern: actors, whenever and wherever they come together, are caught up in the process of differentially applying rights and obligations to one another. Individuals are active constructors of uniquely formulated socio-legal-moral worlds of experience. In this sense, Petrazycki took the study of law out of courtrooms and away from lawyers and legal scholars and placed it squarely inside the province of the sociologist. In a distinctive fashion he anticipated and answered Hoebel's[42] question: "When is a law a law?" His answer was clear-cut: a rule is a law when it establishes a bilateral set of rights and obligations between two or more actors. A rule is simply a moral prescription when it gives obligations but not rights.

Petrazycki took law and its study directly into the realm of focused, face-to-face interaction. But more important, he proposed that intimate relationships could be studied as specialized socio-legal worlds of involvement. Thus, while most scholars would argue that marriages are moral, not legal, concerns, Petrazycki argued:

> jurists traditionally say that relationships between husband and wife—and between parents and children—are regulated by morality and not by law. However, from the point of view of the psychological theory of law as imperative-attributive experiences, family and domestic life (regardless of whether or not there are between those participants any bonds officially recognized) is a broad and peculiar legal world which is awaiting investigation: a legal world with innumerable legal norms, obligations, and rights independent of what is written in the statutes, and solving thousands of questions unforeseen therein . . . each family is a unique legal world, and each of those taking part in domestic life (including aunts, grandmothers, poor kinsfolk in remote degree, or friends received into the house and into the family, hangers-on, adopted and foster children, and the like) has his own particular position in the legal mentality which prevails in that family—the right to enjoy one's room and certain other objects alone and to take part in . . . common meals and pleasures in family celebrations and the like, the right of a decisive or advisory voice in certain matters of domestic life (economic and personal), the right to certain degrees of civility, love, and gratitude and to appropriate behavior in different cases, and so forth.[43]

Social relationships are shifting moral concerns. They are held together over time through mutually felt and agreed upon common understandings. While seldom formalized into legal contracts, these understandings nonetheless act as lawful prescriptions for action. Law surfaces in the most mundane and the most routinized of settings: the home and its domestic order. That order is a negotiated, politically based production. Petrazycki's insight was to see that law—bilateral rights and obligations—infuses every element of the domestic order. Students of family interaction have seldom viewed husband-wife-parent-child relationships from this perspective.[44]

Petrazycki's first contribution to the study of focused interaction was to open up the unresearched field of family or domestic law. His second major contribution was to focus on intimate relationships as another area deserving serious study:

> [This is] the province of intimate relationships between persons close to each other—united by ties of sex or otherwise (fraternity, love, friendship, or joint family life, and so forth). In general this sphere of life and conduct is outside the area of regulation and intervention on the part of statutes, courts, and so forth, but from the point of view of the psychological theory of law this province, too, is subject to legal regulation.

> Thus, mutual rights are recognized in the domain of amatory relationships—rights to fidelity, love, and frankness; to defense in case of malicious gossip or other attack by third persons, to support in case of need, and to thousands of other sorts of assistance and service.[45]

There are, then, love laws and laws of friendship. He comments:

> From the moment love is declared on the one side and accepted on the other, the legal relationships of the parties are fundamentally revolutionized and various legal barriers drop. The one who has proposed acquires various rights which he did not theretofore possess, and there are various further facts which are now legally relevant evoking in their turn more or less essential revolutions in the minds of both sides, making legal bonds closer, and creating new rights and obligations.[46]

Love brings both a right and an obligation, a privilege to be granted only after the individual has established his rights to love and be loved. And, once granted, it becomes an obligation that must be upheld if the love relationship is to continue over time. Conventional views of law and love and social structure would not come to this conclusion.[47]

Petrazycki's psychological theory of law led him to examine games and play as another sector of everyday life, one which until most recently has gone unnoticed by sociologists.[48] He argues:

> There are many occupations and relationships which have no serious business character or significance. Rules of games (such as games of cards, checkers, chess, dominoes, lotto, forfeits, bowls, billiards, and cricket) which define who can and should, in what order and how, accomplish the various actions involved therein (the deal of the cards, the making of certain declarations and "leads," the play of the cards, what cards can take others, and so forth) and state the general principles regarding the obligation to observe special preliminary arrangements and payment of what has been lost, all represent, from our point of view legal norms. They are of an imperative-attributive character: the obligations of some appear as the claims of others and not as "free" obligations, and imperative-attributive, normative complexes are the basis of corresponding projections.[49]

Games and gaming behavior, while on the surface appearing to be nonserious concerns, are nonetheless serious, lawful productions. On fun and games Goffman suggests:

> In daily life, games are seen as part of recreation and "in principle devoid of important repercussions upon the solidity and continuity of institutional life." Games can be fun to play, and fun alone is the approved reason for playing them. The individual, in contrast to his treatment of "serious" activity, claims a right to complain about a game that does not

> pay its way in immediate pleasure and, whether the game is pleasurable or not, to plead a slight excuse, such as an indisposition of mood, for not participating. Of course those who are tactful, ambitious, or lonely participate in recreation that is not fun for them, but their later private remarks testify that it should have been. Similarly, children, mental patients, and prisoners may not have an effective option when officials declare game-time, but it is precisely in being thus constrained that these unfortunates seem something less than persons.[50]

It is a privilege to play, but a privilege that carries an obligation as well. To play is to play by the rules of the game. In their unserious moments actors suspend normal conceptions of reality, and produce a fictional world of thought and action that is grounded in the sociolegal rulings of the game. However, that reality is no less serious than the one played out in the worlds of work, business, and politics. To act untowardly in the game, as Goffman observes, is: "To be awkward or unkempt, to talk or move wrongly, is to be a dangerous giant, a destroyer of worlds. As every psychotic and comic ought to know, any improper move can poke through the thin sleeve of immediate reality."[51]

We can revise Petrazycki's notions of nonseriousness and games. In these activities and the moments they provide, actors make and establish claims as serious, fateful selves. They present themselves as persons who can go to and take the action the game offers. Games are serious concerns. Their rules determine the person's short- and long-term moral career. Goffman argues: "When persons go to where the action is, they often go to a place where there is an increase, not in the chances to be taken, but in the chances that they will be obliged to take chances. Should action actually occur it is likely to involve someone *like* themselves, but someone *else*. Where they have got to, then, is a place where another's involvement can be closely watched and vicariously enjoyed."[52] Men can hire scenes and machines which will give them action. In these seemingly inconsequential payments, a person, as Goffman notes, "without social connections can insert coins in skill machines to demonstrate to the other machines that he has socially approved qualities of character. These naked spasms of the self occur at the end of the world, but there at the end is action and character."[53]

If law and morality shape action in gaming exercises, then it can be seen that moments of polite discourse are also influenced by sociolegal conceptions. Petrazycki observes:

> Imperative-attributive experiences are, to a considerable degree, the basis of so-called rules of courtesy and etiquette (*savoir vivre*) and are from the point of view of the established concept of law, nothing but legal norms. Hosts owe guests various signs of attention and courtesy: places

of honor at the table and being served with food before others (to say nothing of the right, in general, of admission to the table and of receiving the food provided, a breach of which would be a most serious and unheard of "crime"), as well as the swift and zealous fulfillment of their requests and wishes, and so forth.[54]

Rules of Conduct and the Law

The foregoing has suggested that Petrazycki's theory of law and morality brings the study of legal activity directly into the sphere of everyday face-to-face interaction. Family law, love law, laws of friendship, laws of games and chance, and rules of etiquette all share one common element: they tie actors into reciprocated exchanges of rights and privileges. To be in the company of another actor, Petrazycki, like Goffman[55] and Simmel,[56] suggests, is to open one's self up to a ritualized exchange of commodities, services, and niceties. It is a privilege to be let into the company of others, a privilege that is often denied the indigent, the aged, the young, and the stigmatized.

Social life is a ritualized production that rests on three levels, or types of rules: legal specifications (as understood by lawyers) which protect actors and their properties; polite-ceremonial rules which protect actors and their occasions; and relationally specific rules which bind actors into the intimate world of love and friendship. Petrazycki's definition of law can be fitted into this three-fold classification. Domestic law describes relationally specific directives, as does love law and laws of friendship. Rules of the game and rules of etiquette are ceremonially specific declarations, and are just as serious and consequential as legal norms (in the lawyers' meaning).

This reformulation lifts Petrazycki to a higher theoretical level, and solves the overriding deficiency in his definition of law and morality. That is, if law is imperative and attributive in character, then, as Petrazycki's examples show, nearly everything and anything is law, or lawlike. To lump into a single category rules of etiquette, book law, family law, and love law is to make the concept of law so broad as to be relatively useless. The above formulation which stresses three levels or types of rules suggests that rules are differentially binding and bilateral in nature. In a fundamental sense legal specifications (as understood by lawyers) are not like ceremonial rules of etiquette, nor are they like family-specific rules concerning such diverse activities as who does the dishes, takes out the garbage, pays the monthly bills, or initiates the sexual act.

Thus, while Petrazycki brings law back into everyday life, his formulations are too abstract and global. Social scientists need a more specific, situationally grounded definition and conception of law and legal behavior. For the moment, Weber's discussion of legitimate order appears useful:

> The legitimacy of an order may be guaranteed or upheld in two principal ways: (1) from purely disinterested motives, which may in turn be (a) purely affectual, consisting in an emotionally determined loyalty; or (b) may derive from a rational belief in the absolute validity of the order as an expression of ultimate values; or (c) may originate in religious attitudes, through the belief in the dependence of some condition of religious salvation on conformity with the order; (2) also or entirely by self-interest, that is through expectations of specific ulterior consequences, but consequences which are, to be sure, of a particular kind.
>
> A system of order will be called *convention* so far as its validity is externally guaranteed by the probability that deviation from it within a given social group will result in a relatively general and practically significant reaction of disapproval. Such an order will be called *law* when conformity with it is upheld by the probability that deviant action will be met with physical or psychic sanctions aimed to compel conformity or to punish disobedience and applied by a group of men especially empowered to carry out this function.[57]

Petrazycki's analysis of all but book or courtroom law, given Weber's distinctions, pertains to the study of conventions and legitimate orders that stand outside the legal and political arenas of any society or social group.

Conclusion

In this essay I have attempted to establish four principal points. First, Petrazycki's theory of law, morality, and psychological activity shares many parallels with pragmatism and symbolic interactionism. Second, while his psychological theory of objects and their meaning was interactionist in tone, his theory of mental-minded behavior was reductionistic and drive-oriented. Hence, his own theory of meaning was contradicted in his psychological theory. Third, these deficiences aside, the major intent of the present discussion was to extract from Petrazycki's discussion of law those points which could be fitted to the study of focused, face-to-face interaction. Hence, the emphasis on his views of love law, friendship, etiquette, and games. His parallels with Goffman were noted, and certain of his formulations on games and play were recast so as to highlight the serious nature of action and games of chance. Finally, it was argued that Petrazycki's defintion of law could be reformulated within a three-fold conception of rules of conduct. This reformulation was intended to more clearly focus Petrazycki's conceptions of law within a Weberian model of legitimate order.

Many questions remain unanswered. While it can be concluded that Petrazycki brings law and morality back into everyday life, the principal question of whose law and whose morality do actors act in terms of remains unanswered.[58] However, his concern for developing a theory of social technology (see Gorecki in this volume) suggests that he was committed to a somewhat utopian vision of the ideal society. In this respect law, for Petrazycki, would be the final mediator of the perfect social order.

[1]Pitirim A. Sorokin, *Sociological Theories of Today* (New York: Harper and Row, 1966).

[2]Nicholas S. Timasheff, *An Introduction to the Sociology of Law* (Cambridge, Mass.: Harvard University Press, 1939), and also "Growth and Scope of Sociology of Law," Howard Becker and Alvin Boskoff, eds., *Modern Sociological Theory in Continuity and Change* (New York: Holt, Rinehart and Winston, 1957), pp. 424-449.

[3]Georges Gurvitch, *Sociology of Law* (New York: Philosophical Library, 1942).

[4]See Herbert Blumer, *Symbolic Interactionism* (Englewood Cliffs, N.J.: Prentice-Hall, 1969); Charles Horton Cooley, *Human Nature and the Social Order* (New York: Charles Scribner, 1922); George Herbert Mead, *Mind, Self and Society* (Chicago: University of Chicago Press, 1934); Erving Goffman, *Relations in Public* (New York: Basic Books, 1971); Alfred Lindesmith, Anselm L. Strauss, and Norman K. Denzin, *Social Psychology* (4th ed.; New York: Holt, Rinehart and Winston, 1975); Jerome G. Manis and Bernard N. Meltzer, eds., *Symbolic Interaction* (2nd ed.; Boston: Allyn and Bacon, 1972); Gregory P. Stone and Harvey Farberman, eds., *Social Psychology through Symbolic Interaction* (Waltham, Mass.: Ginn-Blaisdell, 1970).

[5]This has been attempted elsewhere. See Pitirim A. Sorokin, *Society, Culture and Personality* (rev. ed.; New York: Cooper Square Publishers, 1962); Nicholas S. Timasheff, "Introduction," *Law and Morality: Leon Petrazycki*, trans. Hugh W. Babb (Cambridge: Harvard University Press, 1955), pp. XVII-XXXVIII; and Jan Gorecki and Jerzy Lande, in this volume.

[6]See Mead, *Mind, Self and Society;* Blumer, *Symbolic Interactionism;* Anselm L. Strauss, *Mirrors and Masks* (San Francisco: Sociology Press, 1969).

[7]See further elaboration of the methodological position of symbolic interactionism in Norman K. Denzin, *The Research Act* (Chicago: Aldine, 1970), and "The Logic of Naturalistic Inquiry," *Social Forces*, 50 (1971), 166-182, and "Theory, Methods and the Observational Act," *Sociale Wetenschappen*, 16e, no. 2 (1973), 75-86.

[8]See Mead, *Mind, Self and Society.*

[9]See Barney G. Glaser and Anselm L. Strauss, *The Discovery of Grounded Theory* (Chicago: Aldine, 1967).

[10]See Charles Horton Cooley, "The Roots of Social Knowledge," *American Journal of Sociology*, 32 (1926), 57-59; Mead, *Mind, Self and Society*, pp. 1-41; George Herbert Mead, "The Psychology of Punitive Justice," *American Journal of Sociology*, 23 (1917), 557-602, reprinted in Andrew J. Reck, ed., *Selected Writings: George Herbert Mead* (Indianapolis, Ind.: Bobbs-Merrill, 1964), pp. 212-247.

[11]Georg Simmel, *The Sociology of Georg Simmel*, trans. Kurt Wolff (New York: Free Press, 1950).

[12]Petrazycki, *Law and Morality*, p. 7.

[13]*Ibid.*

[14]*Ibid.*, p. 8

[15]*Ibid.*, and see Timasheff, "Growth and Scope of Sociology of Law," pp. 425-433.

[16]Mead, "The Psychology of Punitive Justice."

[17]*Ibid.*, pp. 219-220.

[18]Petrazycki, *Law and Morality*, p. 15.

[19]Mead, *Mind, Self and Society*, pp. 7-8.

[20]See, for example, Blumer, *Symbolic Interactionism.*

[21]Petrazycki, *Law and Morality*, p. 13.

[22]*Ibid.*

[23]*Ibid.*

[24]Herbert Blumer, "Comment," *Berkeley Journal of Sociology*, 9 (1964), 118-122.

[25]Max Weber, *The Theory of Social and Economic Organization*, trans. A. M. Henderson and Talcott Parsons (New York: Oxford University Press, 1947), pp. 94-96. Quotations are taken from the 1964 Free Press edition.

[26]George Herbert Mead, *Movements of Thought in the Nineteenth Century* (Chicago: University of Chicago Press, 1936), pp. 390-391.

[27]Petrazycki, *Law and Morality*, p. 23.

[28]*Ibid.*, p. 22.

[29]*Ibid.*

[30]*Ibid.*, p. 23.

[31]*Ibid.*, pp. 23-24.

[32]*Ibid.*, pp. 25-26.

[33]*Ibid.*, p. 26.

[34]*Ibid.*

[35]*Ibid.*

[36]*Ibid.*, p. 27.

[37]*Ibid.*, pp. 49-51.

[38]George Casper Homans, "Bringing Men Back in," *American Sociological Review*, 29 (1964), 809-818. Also Petrazycki, *Law and Morality*, pp. 64-65.

[39]*Ibid.*, p. 46.

[40]*Ibid.*, p. 47.

[41]Timasheff, "Growth and Scope of Sociology of Law," pp. 446-447, makes this point, and compares Petrazycki's work with the theories of Malinowski and Linton.

[42]E. Adamson Hoebel, "Law and Anthropology," *Virginia Law Review*, 32 (1946), pp. 836-854.

[43]Petrazycki, *Law and Morality*, p. 68.

[44]An important exception is Willard W. Waller, *The Old Love and the New: Divorce and Readjustment* (Philadelphia, Pa.: Horace Liveright, Inc., 1930). Also see Ralph Turner, *Family Interaction* (New York: John Wiley and Sons, 1970), and the essay by Gerald D. Suttles, "Friendship as a Social Institution," George J. McCall, *et al.*, eds., *Social Relationships* (Chicago: Aldine, 1970).

[45]Petrazycki, *Law and Morality*, p. 67.

[46]*Ibid.*

[47]See, for example, William J. Goode, "The Theoretical Importance of Love," *American Sociological Review*, 24 (1959), 37-48.

[48]See Erving Goffman, *Encounters* (Indianapolis, Ind.: Bobbs-Merrill, 1961), and *Interaction Ritual* (Chicago: Aldine, 1967).

[49]Petrazycki, *Law and Morality*, p. 64-65.

[50]Goffman, *Encounters*, p. 17.

[51]*Ibid.*, p. 18.

[52]Goffman, *Interaction Ritual*, p. 269.

[53]*Ibid.*, pp. 269-270.

[54]Petrazycki, *Law and Morality*, p. 65.

[55]Goffman, *Interaction Ritual.*

[56]Simmel, *The Sociology of Georg Simmel.*

[57]Weber, *Theory of Social and Economic Organization*, pp. 126-127.

[58]See Maureen E. Cain, *Society and the Policeman's Role* (London: Routledge and Kegan Paul, Ltd., 1973), pp. 21, 246, for some remarks on this issue.

CHAPTER
6
Leon Petrazycki and the Post-Realistic Jurisprudence

ALEXANDER PECZENIK

Petrazycki's Legal Theory

Leon Petrazycki had the courage to think for himself and to make his own mistakes. For this reason he was misunderstood, attacked, or ignored by his contemporaries. Today, however, in part due to changes in scientific fashion, Petrazycki's posthumous popularity is increasing. Nevertheless, I do not think that anything is to be gained by accepting his legal theory as a whole, if only because, like all genuine thinkers, he was inclined to be rather one-sided in his opinions. What we should do is to select some of Petrazycki's ideas, using them in our own frame of reference. That is the intent of this chapter.

Petrazycki's views can be summarized as follows:

(a) *Criticism of jurisprudence.* According to Petrazycki, jurisprudence (that is, legal theory) dealing solely with what the lawyer regards as "valid law" cannot be an adequate theory. Only adequate theories were regarded by Petrazycki as correct and scientifically acceptable. He defined an adequate theory as being neither jumping nor lame. A jumping theory is too wide: what is true about only part of a class is said of the whole. Example: "All soldiers are heroes." A lame theory is too narrow: what is true about the whole class is said only of its part. Example: "All Smiths are mortal."[1] Both the lame and the jumping theories should be eliminated from science, more specifically from the theory of law, to be replaced by adequate theories. The concept "valid law" (in Petrazycki's terminology "official law") covers two different things: the internal law of a state and international law. For that reason, the lawyer's theories are jumping ones; they refer to both categories of law when they are true about only one of them, either about internal law or about international law. Furthermore, the lawyer's theories are also lame; what can be said about "official law" also applies to such phenomena as the internal rules of some private organizations (for example, the Mafia). In this way, the concept "official law" cannot be used in an adequate theory of the law. In order to build a proper theory of the law, the concept "the law" must be redefined so that it will denote a more uniform class of phenomena.[2]

(b) *Psychology*. Petrazycki's psychology was based on a new classification of psychical phenomena. Apart from feeling, knowing, and willing, there exist so-called impulsions. They are active-passive. An example is hunger: it is felt (passively), while at the same time one wants to eat (actively). Especially interesting are the so-called ethical impulsions, which are further divided into moral and legal ones. Moral impulsions consist of the "feeling" that one has a duty, combined with an active, let us say, "readiness" to do one's duty. Legal impulsions consist of the same "feeling" and "readiness," combined with the "feeling" that someone else has a right to the duty being done. If I feel that I ought to give a beggar a dime, this is a moral impulsion. If I feel that I ought to give my creditor one hundred dollars and that my creditor has a right to receive one hundred dollars, this is a legal impulsion.[3] One can thus experience two kinds of legal impulsions: one's own rights in connection with another person's duties, or vice versa: one's own duties in connection with another person's rights.

(c) *Legal theory*. Legal impulsions are the only legal phenomena upon which an adequate theory can be built. Therefore, a correct legal theory must be a psychological one. Petrazycki also infers a terminological conclusion from this: legal impulsions are the only real phenomena which may be called "the law" in the strict scientific meaning of the word. If the term "the law" is extended to apply to something else, for example, the statutes, then the term cannot be used in an adequate theory of law.

Legal rules and norms are nothing more than "impulsive phantasmata" which serve to express legal impulsions without actually describing anything else.

Legal impulsions can be studied and described by means of introspection. This implies that an observer can only study his own legal impulsions. With regard to the legal impulsions of others, he can offer an opinion only by means of analogy to his own.[4]

(d) *Official and intuitive law.* The official "valid law" has the same psychical nature as the rules of games and various other social rules. The theory of the so-called valid law can thus be a part of the broader theory of the so-called attributively imperative impulsions, that is, the impulsions of rights and duties. Gangsters' impulsions concerning their "rights" in a gang, as well as children's impulsions concerning their "rights" in a game, are "law" by Petrazycki's definition and should thus be studied within the same legal theory as the "official law" as understood by the lawyer.

(e) *A Social Darwinism.* The theory of biological evolution is also applicable to human society, that is, to our psychical phenomena and to language. Regarding language, Petrazycki writes: "By processes which, in a way, are similar to natural selection in Darwin's meaning . . . the linguistic terms become brilliantly although unconsciously adapted to the proper orientation among phenomena, and to the correct formulation and communication of information."[5] The brilliant adaptation of a language to its social function is strongest in the case of ordinary language. The language used in professional law is adapted to its practical function in economic life and in the courtroom, rather than to scientific legal theory. Such a theory requires a new, psychologically oriented language.

(f) *A theory of social and legal progress.* By analyzing various historical examples, Petrazycki reached the conclusion that the claims the legal order holds on an individual are increasing continually, whereas legal sanctions decrease continually. The ultimate effect of the evolution would be reached when everybody would observe quite voluntarily even the most demanding legal rules. In this way, the law evolves toward the ideal of the Active Love of Neighbor.[6]

(g) *Legal policy.* As a whole, Petrazycki regarded his own theory merely as an introduction to the science of legal policy, which would be a practical application of the psychological theory of law in the same sense as medicine is a practical application of biology. Knowing the psychological nature of the law, the lawmaker can foresee human reactions to a given statute and to a given kind of legal practice. Thus, he will be able to create norms both efficacious and progressive in the sense of leading the people toward the Active Love of Neighbor.

(h) *A theory about doctrinal study of law.* The doctrinal study of law (German: *Rechtsdogmatik*) makes the law more uniform and better adapted to its social function.[7] Petrazycki's views on doctrinal study of law will be discussed below.

Petrazycki as a Predecessor of Many Modern Theories

Literature about Petrazycki is scarce. The greater part of it, in Polish, is for that very reason inaccessible in international discussion. It is not my intention to make a survey of the literature. Instead, I will present some comments, positive as well as negative, as formulated by some arbitrarily chosen writers.

First, some positive comments. Several authors have pointed out the advantages of Petrazycki's conception of legal policy.[8] Kazimierz Opałek emphasized the fact that Petrazycki formulated some points which were later rediscovered by others. I will quote some examples which may give the well-informed reader some ground for future reference. However, they may be ignored by those whose object is to follow the present paper rather than to get a critical orientation to Petrazycki's theory as a whole. According to Opałek, Petrazycki first discovered several points concerning the following subjects: the pragmatic function of norms, post-decisional dissonance, the informatory function of law, the internal norms of illegal organizations, some important aspects of learning theory and topological theory, the organizational and distributive function of law, the main trends in the historical evolution of law, and so on.[9] Also, Jerzy Wróblewski pointed out that Petrazycki, far ahead of the others, formulated some points concerning the influence of language upon our views (that is, on our concept of *Weltanschauung*).[10] Finally, Jan Woleński observed some parallels between Petrazycki's methodology and Karl Popper's hypothetical-deductive philosophy of science.[11]

The Criticism of Petrazycki's Theory in Literature. Anti-Criticism, the Weakest Point of the Theory

At the same time, many important parts of Petrazycki's theory have been severely criticized, or at least regarded as exaggerated, one-sided, and so on. A typical example of one of Petrazycki's ideas which has been partially accepted and partially rejected in the literature is his concept of adequate theory.[12] I cannot go into detail as regards that form of criticism of Petrazycki. Personally, I believe that Petrazycki was right only to a limited extent. One should not construct jumping theories, since they are false. On the other hand, theories should be constructed as generally as possible, since a general theory is a tool of an economical (that is, concise and elegant) description of reality. Consequently, lame theories should be avoided, because they are uneconomical. Contrary to Petrazycki, however, I believe that lame theories, not being false, are better than none at all. This means that, in the case of practical difficulties precluding the construction of an adequate theory, one should construct a lame one. Furthermore, it means that Petrazycki's criticism of nearly all theories of law as lame ones is exaggerated.[13]

Another very important aspect of the criticism of Petrazycki's theory concerns his rejection of the concept "valid law" (this will be discussed below). Partial approval and partial criticism of Petrazycki's theory are expressed, for example, in the works of N. S. Timasheff[14] and S. Gurvitch.[15] Both authors, who follow Petrazycki's theory in many aspects, criticize his views as being individual-psychological, and they propose a reformulation from the sociopsychological point of view.

It is not my intention to comment on or discuss the opinions of those who regard Petrazycki's views as being exaggerated, over-individualized, one-sided, and so on. However, I must at least present some fragmentary comments upon the latter issue. In this respect, I refer to Karl Olivecrona's criticism of Petrazycki: "The ideas of rights and duties are certainly realities, and so are the powerful emotions connected with them. But the printed figures in books called codes are also real things; this is, of course, also the case with legislative acts, with courts and prisons, etc. In a naturalistic explanation of the realities covered by the term law, all those facts and many others have their place; nothing at all is gained by singling out a specific group among them as the reality of law."[16]

Besides, "the official law as defined . . . by Petrazycki . . . cannot be reduced to psychical experiences."[17] This argument, that Petrazycki's theory is one-sided, has been expressed by nearly all of his critics, for example, Opałek.[18] However, the problem is much more complex than it seems to be. It is unclear whether the above quoted criticism was meant to be interpreted ontologically or methodologically. If ontologically, then the criticism should read thus: "Petrazycki was wrong because he believed that only legal impulsions are real, while in fact also such social phenomena as law books, prisons, etc., are real." This is obviously unfounded, because Petrazycki never claimed that such social phenomena as law books, prisons, and so on, are not real. On the other hand, as a methodological argument the criticism is probably quite sound: "Petrazycki was wrong because he believed that legal impulsions are the only phenomena which can be studied scientifically, while in fact such phenomena as the state organization can also be studied scientifically." This appears to be a sound observation: one can certainly attempt to study scientifically other legal phenomena than legal impulsions.

Petrazycki's overstatement that nothing legal can be studied but the legal impulsions is a consequence of his exaggerated expectations of the scientific method. He demanded that every scientific theory be adequate. At the same time, he observed that no traditional discussion was an adequate general theory. Hence, all legal discussions and studies were inferior to the psychological theory. This was an overstatement, because even non-adequate and non-general theories can be true, interesting, and useful, and in that sense, scientific. Moreover, his own theory, scientific from the point of view of adequacy, is unscientific from the point of view of verification.

The last problem is the most important one. Petrazycki was able, by his psychological theories, to explain nearly all facts known about the evolution of law. His way of writing, and his ability to criticize his adversaries, bear the hallmark of true genius. His ability to discover new points of view, far ahead of anyone else, was quite unbelievable. However, none of this could ultimately save his theory. The main reason was that introspective psychology probably does not fulfill the conditions which, according to modern philosophy of science, must be satisfied by any rigorous scientific theory. Petrazycki, who attacked everybody else for being unscientific, seems to be unscientific himself at the crucial point: there is no sure method to confirm his hypotheses in such a way that an objective observer would be forced to accept them. His theory, based on introspection, is the private theory of Leon Petrazycki, reporting his own legal impulsions, which are not necessarily identical with anybody else's legal impulsions. At the same time, the theory is presented by the author as a general one, applying to the legal impulsions of any individual. This is controversial. First of all, nobody is able to study another person's impulsions directly. At the most, a scientist is able to study another person's behavior and assess his impulsions, but still it is only a guess. Granted, everybody has legal impulsions to some extent similar to Petrazycki's. However, the problem is that the similarity is never absolute. It is always only partial, and no direct method exists to assess the extent of the similarity. Petrazycki's theory is like a brilliant piece of literary art: it can be understood, it may be admired, and—first and foremost—it helps us to understand the facts we know; but it cannot be proven true, and it cannot help us to discover new facts. Still, Petrazycki's theory might enrich modern legal sociology when combined with modern sociological methods such as indirectly guessing (reconstructing) another person's impulsions (or attitudes) from his behavior.

Petrazycki on the Doctrinal Study of Law

Petrazycki's views on the doctrinal study of law are very seldom discussed. It is commonly held that Petrazycki considered doctrinal study of law a quite unscientific activity. Therefore, Petrazycki is often looked upon as a "spiritual relative" of many "realistic" and nihilistic doctrines which reject the cold study of valid law and emphasize the role of free decision-making. However, such a view of Petrazycki is erroneous. Before attempting to bear this out we must emphasize that, due to the importance to lawyers of the doctrinal study of law, the issue is essential. The doctrinal study of law has two main tasks: to interpret legal rules and to systematize them.[19]

(a) A legal impulsion is two-sided: it pertains not only to a duty, but also to a right. A person thinks that others ought to respect his rights. Consequently, a person whose rights are respected has no reason to be grateful, while a person whose rights are not respected is unhappy. He resents those who do not respect his rights, wants to retaliate, and so forth. Not so in the realm of morals. A moral impulsion is one-sided: it does not pertain to a right. Consequently, a person who profits because others fulfill their moral duties is grateful; on the other hand, a person who does not profit in such a way (because others do not fulfill their moral duties) feels no resentment. To be brief: the legal psyche is aggressive, while the moral psyche is nonaggressive.

(b) The content of moral impulsions can differ from one person to another. In the case of peaceful morality, such differences are negligible. However, in the case of aggressive law this situation may create conflicts. Therefore, there is a trend to unify the legal impulsions of different people: when one person feels he has a right to something, the other person feels that he has a corresponding duty.

(c) Positive law is a result of that trend toward uniformity. Before a law becomes positive (that is, when it is merely intuitive), people recognize rights and duties on account of their being just. When the law becomes positive, people begin to recognize rights and duties on other grounds; that is, so-called "normative facts" having taken place, for example, a statute being enacted or a legal custom established. In this sense, even rules of various games, rules of a dance, and so on, are positive. However, the central part of positive law consists of official law, enacted and sanctioned by the state.

(d) The trend toward uniformity also entails a tendency to create clear statutes, as well as a tendency to let others decide when a conflict occurs. Hence we have courts, arbitration, and so forth.

(e) In that context, we can understand Petrazycki's statement: "The essence and the meaning of the scientific (*sic*) doctrinal study of law as a separate special activity and corresponding technique, capable of the unconsciously correct adaptation, can be found in an additional unifying of positive law . . . in working out, on grounds of that law, a system of statements, that will satisfy the need of making legal relations uniform, objectively defined and impartial—(all that) in a more perfect and more complete way than the law itself."[20] The above reasoning, explaining the need to unify the law, is based on Petrazycki's view that the law consists of imperative-attributive impulsions. However, the need for unification can be explained even without resorting to that complex psychological theory. Suffice it to take the argument one step further: that is, to state simply that the most important social rules must be sanctioned by the state because they protect such significant interests that, lacking a sanction, people will attack each other. The controversial assumption that the law consists of two-sided, imperatively attributive impulsions, whereas morality consists of those one-sided, is unnecessary in this context. The general psychological assumptions hence become nothing more than caryatids, apparently bearing, and in fact borne by, the detailed discussion.[21] So much about the need to unify the law. The statement that the need is satisfied, that is, that the doctrinal study of law actually unifies the law, is justified in Petrazycki's theory by the following observations:

(1) The lawyer often performs a so-called "critique" and an interpretation of law.

(2) The "critique" consists of two parts: the first is the statement that a given fact has legal importance, that is, that a given legal text is a legal code; the second is a differentiation between the spheres of application of normative facts of different types, in order not to give rise to any conflict between them.[22]

(3) Interpretation (for example, the construction of statutes) consists in "making explicit the thoughts implicit in a statute," in making legal terms more accurate, in supplying examples for the meaning of those terms, and in constructing hypothetical decisions for possible difficult cases. "In that context the unconscious tendency to unify at any price, to remove possible dissonances and conflicts at all costs, often

leads to . . . a tendentious argument with the properties of sophistry (in its nature innocent and unintentional)." A lawyer who realizes that a given set of legal rules are incompatible with one another tries to remove the incompatibility. "If the main purpose consisted of an objective, historical study of the content of statutes, etc., the doctrinal study of law would often be forced to admit the incompatibility of various details in different statutes. . . . However, the lawyer regards such conclusions as absolutely inadmissible, and does not recognize the facts leading up to them."[23]

(4) A scientific elaboration of the law in the strict sense of the word consists in a generalization of "legal concepts and statements" (based on "critique" and interpretation), and in logical reasonings from those generalizations to new concrete statements which are useful in making decisions in cases not regulated by the statutes. In this way, a lawyer removes the possibilities of conflict while facilitating the unification of law.[24]

(5) "The ultimate method of unification is analogy," that is, *analogia legis* and *analogia iuris*.[25]

These points led Petrazycki to conclude: "The system of legal statements, created by doctrinal study of law through an authoritative-scientific (*sic*) impartial endeavor disregarding personal interests . . . minimizes the possibility of incompatible individual views and conflicts . . . and therein lies the important function of doctrinal study of law."[26] Petrazycki's following views must also be considered: "The doctrinal study of law—because of the strict precision of its concepts, absolute deductive consequence in its reasoning, and method to justify its statements, is similar to mathematics."[27] Moreover, the doctrinal study of law should not adapt itself to "new ideas," such as a discussion of "various persons and their interests." Nor should the doctrinal study of law adapt itself to legal policy, which has different tasks and different methods.[28]

Petrazycki was opposed to any reform of the doctrinal study of law in line with "fashionable slogans." He was also opposed to teleological construction of statutes, as this involved interpreting those statutes according to the interpreter's concept of "the purpose of the statute." Such a reformed, teleological study of law would be "a hypocritical slave, openly cheating his master, and explaining his words (i.e., statutes) according to his own convenience."[29] But at the same time, Petrazycki regarded the doctrinal study of law as a practical science, falling short of the postulate of adequacy as well as being unscientific in the most important, that is, theoretical, sense of the word. It is only in a different meaning that Petrazycki considers the doctrinal study of law to be science.

Legal Realism: A "Realistic" Criticism of Petrazycki's Views Concerning Doctrinal Study of Law. Anticriticism

The above described views have not been adapted to the fashionable idea that only "the law in action," that is, the activity of the courts, is important, while "the law on the books," for example, statutes, is negligible. This idea has been in vogue ever since Holmes wrote his famous slogan: "The prophecies of what the courts will do in fact, and nothing more pretentious, are what I mean by law."[30] From this idea, many versions of *legal realism* have been generated, all of which will not be dealt with here as they are quite well-known and not really relevant to our subject. However, it may be of some interest to quote a few examples.

According to the German *Freirechtschule*, especially in the version of Herman Kantorowicz and Ernst Fuchs, the construction of statutes should follow its linguistic meaning only when the meaning is absolutely clear.[31] In any other case, a judge is, and indeed should be, completely free in his interpretation of a statute. He has to interpret the law according to his own feeling and even his own intuition when deciding which interest should be legally protected. According to an American scholar, J. C. Hutcheson, Jr., the crucial factor in judicial decision-making is the judge's reaction to fact. Irrational and emotional, but nonetheless decisive in a trial, is the judge's hunch, not a given statute or a formal doctrine of *stare decisis.*[32] According to the German Theodor Viehweg,[33] judicial decision-making, including the construction of statutes, is grounded in unclear rhetorical arguments (*topoi*), while logical reasoning from the statutes is without any importance.

All these writers, and many others representing a wide variety of different schools, are unanimously agreed that a judge, to a very great extent, is free in his decision-making. Consequently the doctrinal study of law, based upon statutes, is a mere fiction, not corresponding in the least to "what courts do in fact." Obviously, if all those "legal realists" are right, then Petrazycki is wrong: his concept that the doctrinal study of law, being quite as rigorous as the study of mathematics, is able to unify the law must be false when judges simply ignore the doctrinal study of law and, instead, follow their hunches or their intuition or are persuaded by rhetoric. Neither hunches nor intuition nor rhetoric can facilitate the unification of law. On the contrary.

Quite naturally, Petrazycki's views on the doctrinal study of law have been subject to strong criticism by one of the Polish "legal realists," J. Zajkowski. His criticism was based upon the following observation: Petrazycki believed that the objective meaning of a statute can be discovered. According to Zajkowski, Petrazycki was wrong because there is no such thing as objective meaning.[34]

Actually, Petrazycki was much nearer the truth than his "realistic" critic. It is doubtful whether Zajkowski would admit that his own paper (written in the same ordinary language as the statutes) was meaningless. One cannot forbid others to understand the statutes, while at the same time expecting them to understand one's own comments written in the very same language. However, let us discuss the problem in detail. Zajkowski tries, in fact, to reconstruct Petrazycki's views about the doctrinal study of law, especially about the construction of statutes. His purpose is to adapt Petrazycki's views to legal realism. The starting point of the reconstruction is the following set of propositions, ascribed to Petrazycki: "Legal rules are the convictions of people who experience legal impulsions. Those convictions are subjective. The same statute can motivate different convictions, depending on the people and the circumstances. There are no objective rules. The statutes themselves are products of somebody's legal impulsions, and expressions of somebody's convictions. To every statute there correspond past, present, and future, compatible and incompatible, convictions of various people and nothing else." Those convictions are the only valid legal rules, that is, the subjective rules. "The purpose of the construction of statutes can consist only in discovering those subjective norms." Moreover, that purpose "can be limited to discovering those norms, which are expressed in *communis opinio* of most lawyers, with the judges of the highest courts . . . at the head."[35]

Zajkowski's reconstruction of Petrazycki's views is neither necessary nor useful. There is actually no reason whatever for the person who performs the construction of statutes to produce and express his own legal impulsions. What he should do is attempt to guess the legal convictions experienced by the lawmaker. Petrazycki suggests the latter, Zajkowski, the former. Petrazycki thus suggests a subjective construction of statute, Zajkowski, a nihilistic one. Both are compatible with the rest of Petrazycki's theory. However, only the first—the original version of Petrazycki—is conducive to understanding the unifying function of doctrinal studies of law. Zajkowski's "amendments" preclude this understanding, because substituting the interpreter's own impulsions for the statute does not serve unification. Finally: why should a legal theoretician (for example, Zajkowski) find it easier to discover the rules (resp. convictions) expressed in *communis opinio* of the judges, rather than the rules (resp. convictions) expressed by the lawmaker in the statutes themselves? The only way to learn the *communis opinio* is to read written documents, like precedents, and so forth. Must we assume that such documents are easier to understand than the statutes?

To summarize, Petrazycki's views on the doctrinal study of law, despite their connection with the individually psychological theory of law, are not adaptable to "legal realism." In the next part of this paper, I shall attempt to demonstrate that those views are better adaptable to what I call *post-realism*, including my own views on the doctrinal study of law.

The Certain Ground for Doctrinal Study of Law: The Concept of Valid Law

I think that Petrazycki is right and the realists are wrong in evaluating the doctrinal study of law. The fact of the matter is that jurists and judges take into account a great many central points, rather than depending on hunches, intuition, or rhetoric. One of those is the idea of positive (valid) law. In my opinion, the lawyer can easily find out which rules are legally valid. Moreover, one can easily formulate a meaningful theory concerning the criteria which are employed to distinguish between rules which are legally valid and rules which are not. Hence, the doctrinal study of law has a sound starting point for its unifying activity: it can rely upon valid law.[36]

This problem is especially interesting because Petrazycki himself did not believe that valid (positive, official) law is such a certain ground, in any case not for a theory of law. On the contrary, he pointed out that valid law as understood by lawyers is not a class of phenomena about which one can formulate a scientific (adequate) theory. In the first section of this paper, we have already pointed out the reason for this opinion, that is, that the "official law" in the lawyers' meaning is a nonuniform mixture of two quite different things: international law and the internal law of a state. For that reason, a theory of "official" law would be a jumping one: it must refer to both categories of law when it is true about only one of them, either international or internal law. Besides, a theory of "official" law must be lame in other respects: what can be said about "official" (valid) law can also be said about the internal rules of some private organization (such as the Mafia), and so on. Thus, the concept "official law" cannot be used in legal theory.

Petrazycki's skepticism regarding the concept of valid ("official") law has been criticized by Opałek and by Wroblewski. Opałek observes that the theory of valid law can avoid being a jumping one when it separately discusses international law and internal law.[37] Both authors observe that the theory of valid law need not be lame, since it can state a great deal about valid law which is not applicable to, for example, the Mafia. Contrary to Petrazycki's opinion, the property of being valid ("official") law can be defined in an objective, descriptive way.

Neither Opałek nor Wroblewski have, however, elaborated their definitions in detail. Therefore, instead of quoting their brief comments I will use my own reconstruction of the concept "valid law."[38] This reconstruction is based on Kelsen's views, completing them by various "realistic" points. Consequently, it derives a great deal from Kelsen's *Reine Rechtslehre.*

The main points of the reconstruction are as follows: judicial decisions are valid because they satisfy certain conditions formulated by the statutes or by the customary doctrine of the sources of the law. The statutes are valid because they were enacted according to the constitution, and because at some time they satisfy the same conditions formulated by the customary doctrine of the sources of the law. The constitution itself is valid and the doctrine of the sources of the law is acceptable because the legal system grounded on them is, on the whole, efficacious, and because that system shows certain other important marks, such as would be unknown, for example, in the Mafia. Those marks are, for example, that the legal system is broader than the Mafia's system, that it has a claim on the monopoly of force, that it is discussed by professional lawyers, that it generates specific human attitudes, and so on. All this is taken into account when the people decide which normative system is to be called "valid law." It is taken into account because ordinary language contains a linguistic rule that only such a system should be called "valid law." I am unable here to expound further on this theory, but I believe that this solves Kelsen's mystery of *Grundnorm*, as well as difficulties that the "realistic" theory encounters when dealing with some formally valid law which is not applicable by the courts. I have elsewhere discussed the way in which such difficulties are solved.[39]

My view on valid law, briefly outlined above, can be summarized by means of the following diagram, in some respects similar to Kelsen's pyramid of valid rules of greater and lesser importance.

Two additional comments on the diagram are necessary. (1) The customary doctrine of the sources of the law comprises the basic bibliog-

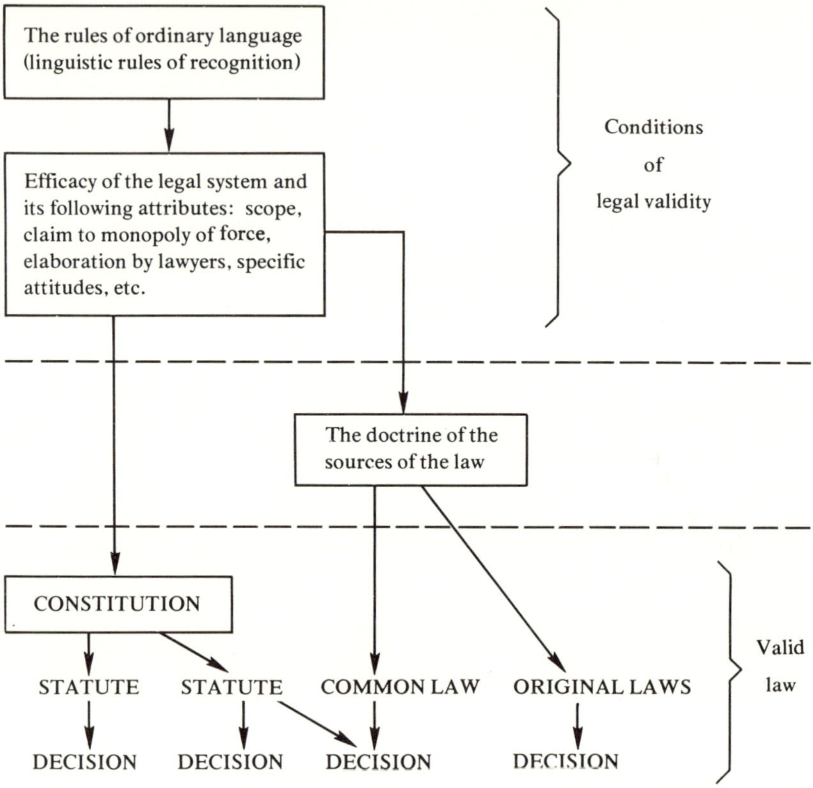

raphy of rules and evaluations which should be taken into account by lawyers. The simplest part of the bibliography is often a starting point of the standard legal education. At the very beginning of his career the future lawyer learns that he should justify his professional opinions by statutes, precedents, legal custom, and so on. At the same time, he learns where to look for statutes, precedents, legal customs, and so on. At law school and in his job, every competent lawyer acquires a great deal of further information about what is to be regarded as the sources of the law. (2) The doctrine of the sources of the law is, in the diagram, located even higher than the constitution. The main reason is the existence of so-called "original laws." Let me quote a Swedish example: *Tryckfrihetsförordningen* 1812 (the statute enforcing the freedom of the press) was during a long period recognized as valid law in spite of its clearly unconstitutional origin. The doctrine of the sources of the law decides that "original laws" are valid even though they had not been made in a way required by the constitution. From that point of view, the doctrine is more important than the constitution. However, by locating the doctrine above the constitution, our diagram becomes open to the following criticism: The doctrine can be changed by a change in the constitution (or even a change in a statute). How, in spite of that, can the doctrine be regarded as "higher" than the constitution? The question can be answered as follows: The doctrine is "higher" in *one* respect—it is used as a justification of the validity of a statute, even if the statute had been enacted in an unconstitutional way. In that sense the hierarchy of the legal system is: linguistic rules, social facts, the doctrine of the sources of the law, the constitution, statutes and precedents, decisions. On the other hand, if we assume that a "higher" rule is to be defined as the rule that can change a "lower" one (but not vice versa), then the hierarchy would, of course, be different: the constitution, statutes and common law, the doctrine of the sources of the law, decisions.

The most important point in the above theory of valid law is that legal validity can be established on the grounds of a set of facts. Granted that the facts are complex in their relationship to one another, but they are facts: efficacy, the legal profession, legislative activity, and so on. This means that the doctrinal study of law is built on a sound factual base.

The Certain Ground for Doctrinal Study of Law: The Customary Rules for the Construction of Statutes. Example: The Choice between Analogy and Reasoning a Contrario

On the certain ground of valid law, the doctrinal study of law formulates several statements. In Continental law, the most important of those statements are the propositions about the "legal meaning" of the statute. Such propositions are formulated in effect to the construction of statutes. In my book, *Juridikens metodproblem*, I have analyzed the bound and free elements in the construction of statutes, reaching, among others, the following conclusions: In order to interpret a statute, a lawyer must make a choice between several permissible interpretations. When making the choice in question, the lawyer uses many methods of interpretation, such as literary interpretation, legal analogy, arguments concerning justice, arguments concerning the lawmaker's intention, arguments concerning precedents, arguments concerning "the purpose of law," and rhetorical arguments. The lawyer uses all of these methods in a variety of combinations; a construction of statutes using only one single method is quite rare. When different methods lead to incompatible conclusions, the lawyer must make a choice, that is, decide which of the methods is preferable in the issue at stake. There are several customarily valid rules which restrict the discussed freedom of choice; rules which probably are quite obvious to the American reader. On the Continent, however, the situation is different. Legal positivism gave rise to the myth that the statute is the only, or almost the only, proper "source of law." The statutes are valid, while the rules for their construction, not being written down in the statutes, are not valid. In conjunction with legal realism, it led many scholars to the conclusion that, in fact, there is no valid law at all, because the statutes (supposed to be valid) are meaningless unless interpreted, and the rules of their interpretation are neither valid nor clear.

I am strongly opposed to such a mixture of legal positivism and legal realism. As the starting point for a justification of my opinion, let us take the statement that even on the Continent there exist (nonstatutory) rules for the construction of statutes. The customarily valid rules of construction are, however, complex and not clear. In order to understand their nature, we will take, for example, the rules for the choice between analogy in law and the so-called *argumentum a contrario*. One of the most important tools for unifying the law is reasoning by analogy. This is essential in the doctrine of *stare decisis*, as well as in the construction of statutes. In the latter context, the reasoning by analogy, as used by lawyers, has been strongly criticized by "legal realism." I will outline this criticism now, and return to Petrazycki's theory later.

Legal tradition concerning the use of analogy in the construction of statutes in Continental law can be described as follows. The main form of analogy in law is *analogia legis*, which can be explicated thus: There is a "gap" in the law. Some cases ought to be regulated by law but are not. "Gaps" can be filled by analogy. Let us assume that no legal norm regulates a given case C. But a given norm, *n*, intuitively read or properly interpreted, requires or permits us to decide some other cases in a given way W. The case C is similar to all these cases or at least to some of them, regarded as typical. The similarity concerns persons or acts, duties, rights, place, time, and so on, and is evaluated as essential. Hence the case C is also decided in the way W, or similarly. The same conclusion is drawn when the decision of the case C would cause similar social effects as decisions of the cases regulated by *n* do. But only some effects are taken into account, evaluated as the proper function of the norm.

The ultimate ground for *analogia legis* is the general principle of justice: essentially similar objects should be treated in a similar way. That principle is first and foremost applied to people. Hence the principle: essentially similar human beings should be treated in a similar way. But the principle "essentially similar cases should be treated in a similar way" also follows from the general principle of justice.[40] The principle of justice, applied to people and to cases, leads to the generalizing of legal rules and to the unifying of law. That process of generalization is similar in some respects to scientific generalization. In science, on the grounds of an observation that some planets have elliptical trajectories, one may conclude that all planets have elliptical trajectories. We can see now that the construction of statutes, *analogia legis*, must lead to the unification of law, exactly the way Petrazycki predicted. The reason is that the construction of statutes, using *analogia*, is similar to a scientific generalization. And, of course, a generalization means a unification. The parallel between generalization in science and justice (analogy) in law is, however, not absolute. The general scientific conclusion ("all planets have elliptic trajectories") is a hypothesis, a guess, which is to be abandoned when a planet is discovered which does not have an elliptic trajectory. In science, false general hypotheses can be proved so if they are incompatible with facts. The question which concerns us now is: Is it possible to prove that a generalization in law, for example, the conclusion that the case C should be treated in the same way as some other similar case, is either true or false? If not, is it possible to prove at least that such a conclusion is right or wrong, correct or incorrect, valid or invalid, and so on? In short, the problem is to find out whether a possible generalization of a statutory rule is right or wrong. Let us discuss the problem more carefully.

When an interpreter refuses to use *analogia legis*, he automatically uses another type of legal reasoning called *argumentum a contrario*. *Argumentum a contrario* consists of the following: a statute should be applied solely to cases which clearly fall under its linguistic meaning; the statute should not be applied to any other case, no matter what analogies are noticed. Many legal realists think that *analogia legis* and *argumentum a contrario* are merely labels, freely used after the "free interpretation" of law is done. They maintain that, since in principle the choice between those labels is free, they are without any value.[41] According to these authors, the processes of generalization in law differ from the process of generalization in science because the former, unlike the latter, cannot be corroborated, and therefore is free, arbitrary, and intuitive. In my opinion, the freedom of choice between *analogia* and *argumentum a contrario* is restricted, however, by legal custom (of interpretation) and by doctrine.[42] These recommend various rules for the choice under discussion. Sometimes pragmatic standards are suggested; for example, in the case of "two opposing rules which are competing for room . . . values and principles embodied in modern statutes should be given more weight than the values and principles of past days."[43] Sometimes legislative history is quoted, and even purely linguistic arguments can be found. This can be illustrated as follows. The Contract Acts of Denmark, Sweden, and Finland, Sec. 32, contains the following provision: A party who has made a promise which, due to a slip of the pen, has obtained a content other than that intended is not bound by its content if the promisee knew or had reason to know of the mistake. As the legislative history clearly indicates, this provision was supposed to justify a conclusion *a contrario*. A mistake is, as a rule, no excuse when the other party does not know, nor has reason to know, of the mistake.[44] Sometimes, *analogia legis* seems to be forbidden, either by statute or by customary law. For example, in many countries it is forbidden to punish anybody on the ground of *analogia legis* from a criminal statute.[45] Besides, according to the principle *singularia non sunt extenda*, norms that constitute exceptions should not be applied extensively, for example, by analogy. In the above mentioned book I give various examples of other customary limitations of the use of *analogia legis*. For example: *analogia* should not be used as the sole justification for creating new legal institutions. *Analogia* should not be used if it leads to the conclusion that the lawmaker has made an outright mistake. *Analogia* should not be used for justifying some new restrictions of freedom or new obligations (*odia non sunt restringenda*), and so on. I cannot discuss the Swedish examples in detail. But the conclusion seems to be clear: the choice between *argumentum a contrario* and *analogia legis* is not absolutely free, but rather it is limited by various rules of construction. None of those rules are clear; none is applied without exception. In spite of that, however, they serve as a kind of guide for the judge in his decision-making and in the construction of statutes.

The Certain Ground for Doctrinal Study of Law: General Remarks on the Customary Rules for the Construction of Statutes

The above remarks about the rules governing the choice between *analogia legis* and *argumentatum a contrario* can be generalized to other rules pertaining to the construction of statutes.

Some of those rules are valid as customary law. Granted, in the Continental system there is no equivalent to the British and American doctrine of binding precedents. In spite of that, a legal theoretician still cannot deny that both precedents and various other nonstatutory forms of the "sources of law" are in a sense valid law, even in Continental legal systems.

Concerning rules pertaining to the construction of statutes, I think that these rules should be regarded, in a sense, as valid law when one of the following facts occurs:

(1) Explicit formulation in a precedent.

(2) Hypothetical application in a precedent.

Such rules of interpretation are not explicit in a precedent, but may be derived by means of the established doctrine of *ratio decidendi*. In both cases, the rules of construction in question should be taken into account by future practice; it is true in the common law countries as well as in Continental Europe. Granted, a European judge disregarding these rules is not guilty of committing any crime. Nevertheless he is, and according to the accepted doctrine of the sources of law he ought to be, exposed to a sanction of a different order: his decision is going to be overruled. For that reason, I wish to say that in the Continental legal system judges have a weak duty to follow precedents and other forms of nonstatutory law.

Some rules of construction are "nearly valid" in view of the following circumstances:

(3) Explicit formulation by many "lower" courts (not having the competence to create binding precedents).

(4) Explicit formulation in doctrine, *travaux préparatoires*, and so on, and a "potential" application by the courts. The courts decide many cases as if they had applied these rules.

Some rules of construction are certainly not legally valid, but they may be used as efficient arguments in legal discourse; the efficiency of such arguments depends on many circumstances. Two special cases of the efficient rules of construction are especially interesting:

(5) "The law behind the law." Some rules of construction are in a way potentially expressed in a statute or in legal practice in spite of the fact that, so far, they have not been formulated in doctrine nor in *travaux préparatoires*. Similarly, as above in item 4, it can be said that a statute is written as if the lawmaker referred to those rules, or judicial decisions are made as if the courts applied them.

(6) The rational justification of rules of construction in another way; for example, by proving that they are concordant with the commonly accepted value statements in a given society.

The efficient (but not valid) rules for the statutory construction can be used by the lawyer as "open," not "bound," arguments. (Only when no such arguments are satisfactory, from the interpreter's point of view, can the question of interpretation be answered completely freely.) The "open" arguments may collide with one another, but together they lead to a compromise. The "correct" construction of statutes is determined by that compromise. However, the compromise is not quite free. To some extent, the construction of statutes is always bound by various rules of construction. The real legal discussion must concern the problem of to what extent it is bound, not the question of whether it is bound or totally free. A judge, and consequently also the doctrinal study of law, is only partially free when interpreting law.

The reason why so many legal theoreticians have not realized the points mentioned above (that is, the cause of the one-sided "realistic" theory of the construction of statutes as a totally free, unpredictable, emotional activity) can probably be found in the old philosophical ideals of absolute truth, absolute security, and absolute precision. The customary rules for the construction of statutes are neither absolutely clear nor absolutely precise. Therefore, some legal philosophers have denied their existence.

As we have pointed out above, Petrazycki regarded the doctrinal study of law both as scientifically exact and, at the same time, as "sophistically" (although "innocently") ignoring facts. I think that there is no contradiction between "science" and "sophistry" in the study of law. The doctrinal study of law is "sophistry," because it interprets the statutes tendentiously in order to adapt them to precedents, *travaux préparatoires*, and so forth. It is "science," because the tendentious interpretation is determined by commonly accepted rules, and, besides, the result of the interpretation is a generalization of law. In other words, the study of law can be placed somewhere between "science" and "sophistry." Petrazycki was, after all, right when he emphasized the non-arbitrary elements in the doctrinal study of law. He was also right in stating that one of the ultimate tasks of the doctrinal study of law is to unify the law, or to make it more just.

It is amazing that Petrazycki's views, formulated at the same time as the very first works of "legal realism," can be used today, sixty years afterward, as an argument in a criticism of that particular school. Most Scandinavian scholars of today are beginning to suspect that the old realism was one-sided and exaggerated. Consequently, the legal scholars, at least in Sweden, quite often refuse to accept any legal philosophy or legal theory at all. This is an old and typical situation when a passé school is to be replaced by a new one. I hope that the negation of the exaggerated parts of legal realism, together with the retention of all that was good and right in that school, will lead in the future to a new school of legal theory, to *post-realism*. I hope that my views, some of which I have expressed above, may become a part of that new school. If our expectations are right, Petrazycki's appeal, at least the appeal of his views on the doctrinal study of law, is increasing.

That is the proof of greatness. Scientific fashion changes nearly as quickly as *haute couture* does. Still, every new school has something to borrow from the truly great thinkers of the past—and especially from Petrazycki.

[1]See Tadeusz Kotarbiński, Chapter 2 of this volume.

[2]See Petrazycki, *Wstep do nauki prawa i moralnosci* (Introduction to the Study of Law and Morality) (Warszawa: P.W.N., 1959), pp. 43-46, 52-58. Compare also his *Teoria prawa i panstwa* (Theory of Law and State) (Warszawa: P.W.N., 1959), vol. 1, pp. 335-342, 349-350.

[3]Petrazycki, *Teoria* (Warszawa: P.W.N., 1960), vol. 2, pp. 5-6.

[4]Petrazycki, *Wstep do nauki prawa i moralnosci*, pp. 61-71.

[5]Petrazycki, *Teoria*, vol. 1, p. 104.

[6]Petrazycki, *Die Lehre vom Einkommen* (Berlin: Verlag von H. W. Müller, 1895), vol. 2, pp. 475-481, and *O ideale spolecznym i odrodzeniu prawa naturalnego* (Warszawa, 1925), *passim*, esp. p. 52.

[7]Petrazycki, *Teoria*, vol. 1, p. 312.

[8]For example, M. Borucka-Arctowa, *O spolecznym dzialaniu prawa* (The Social Function of Law) (Warszawa: P.W.N., 1967), pp. 31-35; K. Opałek, *Problemy metodologiczne nauki prawa* (Methodological Problems of Legal Science) (Warszawa: P.W.N., 1962), pp. 35ff.

[9]K. Opałek, "Teoria Petrazyckiego a wspolczesna teoria prawa" (Petrazycki's Theory and Modern Jurisprudence), in K. Opałek, ed., *Z zagadnien*, pp. 127ff., 130ff.

[10]J. Wróblewski, "Jezyk a nauka w teorii Leona Petrazyckiego" (Language and Sciency in Leon Petrazycki's Theory), in K. Opałek, ed., *Z zagadnien*, p. 186.

[11]J. Woleński, "Metodologiczne dazenia Petrazyckiego a wspolczesna teoria nauki" (Petrazycki's Methodology and Modern Theory of Science), in K. Opałek, ed., *Z zagadnien*, p. 164.

[12]Compare, for example, I. Lazari-Pawłowska, "Tworzenie pojec nauk humanistycznych wedlug koncepcji Leona Petrazyckiego" (Formation of Concepts in Humanities According to Leon Petrazycki), in *Fragmenty Filozoficzne*, ser. 2 (Warszawa: P.W.N., 1959), pp. 102ff. Compare also critical remarks by J. Zajkowski, "Wykladnia ustaw wedlug Petrazyckiego i jego teorii" (Construction of Statutes According to Petrazycki and His Theory), in *Wileński Przeglad Prawniczy* (1936), pp. 11-27, and a positive evaluation by J. Lande, *Studia z filozofii prawa* (Studies on Philosophy of Law) (Warszawa: P.W.N., 1959), pp. 576-583. My own views on adequate theories have been expressed in A. Peczenik, *Wartosc naukowa dogmatyki prawa* (The Scientific Value of the Doctrinal Study of Law) (Kraków: Zeszyty Naukowe U.J., 1966), p. 85.

[13]See W. Lang, "Leona Petrazyckiego krytyka prawa w rozumieniu prawniczym" (Leon Petrazycki's Criticism of the Law as Understood by Lawyers), in K. Opałek, ed., *Z zagadnien*, pp. 63-66.

[14]Nicholas S. Timasheff, *An Introduction to the Sociology of Law* (Cambridge, Mass.: Harvard University Press, 1939), pp. 4, 298.

[15]S. Gurvitch, "Une philosophie intuitive du droit: Leon Petrazycki," *Archives de Philosophie du Droit et de Sociologie Juridique*, 3-4 (1931), p. 403.

[16]K. Olivecrona, "Is a Sociological Explanation of Law Possible?," *Theoria*, XIV/2 (1948), 177-178.

[17]*Ibid.*, p. 178.

[18]Opałek, "Teoria Petrazyckiego," pp. 123ff.

[19]Petrazycki, *Teoria*, vol. 1, pp. 236-329.

[20]*Ibid.*, p. 312.

[21]A famous expression by Somlo.

[22]Petrazycki, *Teoria*, vol. 1, pp. 313-315.

[23]*Ibid.*, pp. 318-322.

[24]*Ibid.*, pp. 322-323.

[25]*Ibid.*, p. 323.

[26]*Ibid.*, p. 326.

[27]*Ibid.*, p. 328.

[28]Petrazycki, *Die Lehre vom Einkommen*, vol. 2, pp. 578-579.

[29]Petrazycki, *Bona fides v grazhdanskom prave* (Bona Fides in Civil Law) (St. Petersburg: N. I. Martinov, 1897), p. 386.

[30]Oliver Wendell Holmes, Jr., "The Path of the Law," *Harvard Law Review*, 10 (1897), 461.

[31]Compare, for example, Gnaeus Flavius (Herman Kantorowicz), *Der Kampf um die Rechtswissenschaft* (Heidelberg: Carl Winter, 1906), *passim.*

[32]Joseph Chappell, Jr., *Judgement Intuitive* (Chicago: The Foundation Press, Inc., 1938), esp. chap. 2.

[33]Theodor Vichweg, *Topik und Jurisprudenz* (München: Beck, 1953), *passim.* Similar, although more carefully expressed, ideas have been formulated by a Belgian scholar, Chaim Perelman; compare Perelman and L. Olbrechts-Tyteca, *La Nouvelle Rhétorique, Traité de l'Argumentation* (Paris: Presses universitaires de France, 1958), *passim.*

[34]Zajkowski, "Wykladnia," pp. 41, 42.

[35]*Ibid.*, pp. 45, 46.

[36]Compare also W. Lang, "Leona Petrazyckiego krytyka," pp. 66-71. Lang emphasizes (on p. 70) that a scientific theory of the law as understood by lawyers is definitely possible.

[37]Opałek, "Teoria Petrazyckiego," p. 132.

[38]*Ibid.*, and Wróblewski, "Jezyk a nauka," pp. 186, 187.

[39]Compare A. Peczenik, "The Concept of 'Valid Law,'" *Scandinavian Studies in Law*, 16 (1972), 213, 251. The second version is formulated in Swedish in my *Juridikens metodproblem* (Stockholm: Almquist and Wiksell, 1974), pp. 44ff.

[40]In American literature, compare, for example, E. H. Levi, *An Introduction to Legal Reasoning* (Chicago: University of Chicago Press, 1963), pp. 1-3, 8-9; see also my *Juridikens metodproblem*, pp. 82, 177ff.

[41]Compare A. Ross, *On Law and Justice* (Berkeley: University of California Press, 1959), pp. 151ff.

[42]Compare A. Peczenik, "Analogy from Statutes in Continental Law," *Proceedings of the World Congress for Legal and Social Philosophy*, Brussels (1971), 3-9, and *Juridikens metodproblem*, pp. 86ff.

[43]F. Schmidt, "Construction of Statutes," *Scandinavian Studies in Law*, 1 (1957), 195, 196.

[44]F. Schmidt, "Model, Intention, Fault. Three Canons for Interpretation of Contracts," *Scandinavian Studies in Law*, 4 (1960), 184.

[45]The prohibition of that kind, in force in many states, is not clear in Sweden, since the Swedish Supreme Court accepts analogy in penal law if there are very strong pragmatic reasons for doing so (comp. Nytt juridiskt arkiv, 1959, p. 254). In any case, even in Sweden, the admissible use of analogy in criminal law is much more restricted than in civil law.

CHAPTER

7

Moral and Legal Norms[1]

MARIA OSSOWSKA

Hundreds of pages have already been written about the difference between legal and moral norms. Some authors have seen the difference in their external form, others in their content, some in their origin, others in the circumstances under which they are binding, or in sanctions applied to those who did not conform themselves to their commands. One of these numerous proposals will be discussed here. It seems particularly attractive and has been largely accepted, not only by jurists but also by social anthropologists studying legal institutions in primitive societies. This proposal had been advocated and treated in the most exhaustive way by Petrazycki.

According to Petrazycki, moral norms are norms which command without authorizing anybody to claim the deed commanded, while legal norms are not just unilaterally binding but give to others a right to claim the fulfillment of the norm. The former are only imperative, while the latter have an imperative-attributive character. This characterization, as the author explains, is not to be treated as a *description* of the existing division of roles in the domain of morality on the one hand, and law on the other, but it constitutes a *proposal* for a demarcation line. This proposal is not a purely conventional one, but it grasps the very nature of law, which has, as yet, not been adequately characterized by theorists. It is only this distinction which makes it possible to formulate adequate theories concerning either morality or law, that is, theories which embrace *all* the objects belonging to the characterized class and refer to these objects *exclusively*.

As mentioned above, this theory is widely known and widely accepted. Referring to Petrazycki, the German jurist, G. Radbruch, accepts the former's distinction as one of the differences between morality and law. "The legal obligor," as he writes in his studies on legal philosophy, "is always confronted with an obligee, an interested claimant, whereas to the moral duty such an obligee is attached only as a symbol when it is called a duty toward one's own conscience, toward humanity in one's own person, toward one's better self. In the field of law one may talk of duty as an obligation that is owed; but the moral duty is not thus owed to a creditor, but is a duty pure and simple."[2] G. del Vecchio in his article, "Homo juridicus," treats this distinction as firmly established. "L'impératif juridique," he writes, "a ceci de particulier par rapport à l'impératif moral, qu'il fait naître un devoir dans un sujet a l'égard d'un autre sujet, et celui-ci, par cet acte même, acquiert la faculté d'exiger que ce devoir soit rempli."[3]

This distinction, clear and convincing at first sight, can be interpreted in different ways, and each of these interpretations, as we shall endeavor to show, encounters difficulties that are not easy to overcome. We shall examine them successively, referring to the writings of Petrazycki and especially to his book *On the Motives of Human Behavior*.

According to the first interpretation, a norm like "Honor thy father and thy mother" would be legal for X if X considered not only that people are under the obligation of honoring their parents, but also that parents are entitled to require it as something due to them. To be entitled to require is, in other words, to have the right to do so or, in still other words, to make justified claims. In fact, in Petrazycki's writings we find on many occasions a distinction of justified and unjustified claims, reasonable and unreasonable demands. It would be absurd, in his opinion, to interpret the rule: "Resist not evil. Whoever shall smite thee on thy right cheek turn to him the other also; and if any man will sue thee at law and take away thy shirt, let him have thy cloak also," as a bilateral rule giving to the offender the right to smite the left cheek or the right to obtain the cloak. Although it would be less absurd to treat the obligation of humility, chastity, and perfection as bilateral, the obligations formulated in the New Testament are generally unilateral and do not allow one to claim from anybody the fulfillment of its ideals.

All those writers who accept Petrazycki's distinction of law and morality also accept his distinction of absurd and reasonable claims. The social anthropologist, Bronislaw Malinowski, adopts, as what he calls the anthropological definition of law, the following formula: "The rules of law stand out from the rest in that they are felt and regarded as the obligations of one person and the rightful claims of another."[4] It is, according to him, the only definition which gives an adequate idea of the function of law in a primitive society.

The use of expressions like "rightful" or "valid claims" seems very dangerous for the definition, since a claim is rightful or valid always in reference to some rules which are tacitly assumed. When somebody holds that parents may not request to be honored by their children or that nobody can claim humility from other people, this "cannot" does not constitute a technical impossibility, like the impossibility of being in two different places at the same time. "Cannot" means here "is in disagreement with a rule treated as self-evident." Bentham already knew very well that the notion of valid claims or rights implied the existence of rules of a higher order. Although he sympathized with the spirit of the "Declaration" of the French Revolution, he could not agree with its form, since the notion of rights, involving a reference to rules, could not, in his opinion, be used as the starting point.

Petrazycki does not usually support by any argument his opinion that a claim in a given case is not valid. Rather exceptionally, when treating the obligation of humility, chastity, and perfection as unilateral, he points to the prejudicial consequences of entitling people to such claims. Claims of this kind would make peaceful conditions impossible within a society, the more so as people are inclined to demand of their neighbors much more than they demand of themselves. Thus in this case Petrazycki thinks it unreasonable to claim humility or perfection from people in view of the tacitly assumed principle of avoiding conflicts between members of a society. A principle of this or of some other kind is always to be found in the arguments of those who consider a claim valid or not. And then the question immediately arises: is this rule of reference moral or legal? This question can be answered only by referring to new principles, necessary for deciding whether it is unilateral or bilateral, that is, connected with valid claims or not. Thus we find ourselves involved in a *regressus* which leads us to infinity, or to a point where, having no more rules of a higher order to refer to, we cannot apply the distinction of moral and legal rules any more.

Let me know, one could say, which claims are valid and which are not, according to your opinion, and it will give me an idea of the ethics you advocate, the distinction of valid and invalid claims being symptomatic of people's moral attitudes. He who thinks that chastity cannot be requested from others reveals either that, according to him, chastity does not always deserve approval, or that we cannot interfere in the private life of our neighbors and that everybody may dispose of his own person as he likes. He who holds that humility cannot be a matter of claim manifests his opinions on what should be the proper relations of man to man. A person approving of a social hierarchy, like the hierarchy of a caste system, would probably have a different view of the subject. The decision, whether the norm, "Honor thy father and thy mother," is legal or moral, would, in conformity with Petrazycki's criteria, depend on the opinion whether symmetrical relations of love and friendship are not preferable in family life to asymmetrical ones, and on the opinion whether the very fact of giving birth to their children entitles parents to claim an attitude of respect which can be due only for personal merits. And whoever treats the claim to smite the other cheek as absurd confesses that the idea contradicts his fundamental concepts of human dignity.

The use of the concept of valid claim does not necessarily involve a reference to moral principles. In judging a claim absurd or unreasonable, people may refer also to legal rules, rules of custom, or technical principles. Thus, for example, he who denies the right of parents to be honored may refer to the fact that emotions are spontaneous and cannot be felt on command. But the very fact that the concept of a valid claim usually implies reference to moral or legal norms renders the use of this concept impossible in the definition of law.

Let us now consider another interpretation of the concept of valid claim, which can also be derived from Petrazycki's writings as well as from the writings of those theorists who share his opinions.

According to Petrazycki, the fact that moral norms are only imperative, while legal ones are imperative and attributive, is not necessarily expressed in the formal structure or the content of a norm, since norms usually have an elliptical form. The distinction is ultimately a *psychological* one, and it is impossible to class a norm either as legal or as moral, without knowing the state of mind of the person who makes use of it, the norm being legal when connected with a bilateral "impulsion," and moral when the impulsion is only unilateral.

By adopting this psychological point of view, we may give a different interpretation to the concept of a valid claim: a claim can be considered valid not with reference to certain principles but with reference to some sociopsychological fact, namely, the fact of being widely experienced in the given group. In this case, a norm recommending action A would be legal when used by X if X felt not only an obligation to perform A, but also the pressure of claims on the part of his fellow men, these claims being sufficiently widely shared to be treated as justified and not as a matter of individual caprice. This reference to claims as social facts gives to the psychological definition of Petrazycki a certain stability, since the person obliged has his counterpart in another person, not imaginary but real, who requires the action recommended by the norm and is in his claims supported by other members of the group. Petrazycki himself often interpreted his distinction in that way, for example, when he was stressing the pressure of social claims upon the mind of individuals or when he described the social evolution of norms. Whenever people became conscious of their rights, whenever, according to Petrazycki's expression, their mind freed itself from servitude, unilateral norms were transformed into bilateral ones, a social process which he considered not only as evolution but also as progress.

By interpreting in this way the distinction of legal and moral norms, we avoid the danger of defining valid claims by referring to norms of a higher order. But since the validity of claims is here ascertained by their very existence, the notion of claim itself must be clear enough to enable us to decide whether in a given case we have to do with a claim of this sort or not. This notion was not so important when the claim could only be imagined and when the only thing which mattered was whether it was considered valid, from the point of view of certain assumed principles. Now it can be valid only when real and commonly shared.

The notion of claim is certainly not simple, and what seems particularly interesting to a moral scientist is to clarify its relation to moral disapproval. Does not any claim contain a potential disapproval, in case it is not complied with? And does not any moral disapproval imply a claim? He who claims from his employer a two-week leave after a year of hard work will disapprove of the refusal. Inversely, does not he who disapproves of his friend, who has deserted his wife and children, claim a different behavior? For some theorists, for example, E. Westermarck, moral disapproval is always an expression of resentment, and the concept of resentment seems very closely related to that of claim.

These questions being as yet unanswered, the denotation of the term "claim" must be treated as rather vague. It is a well-known fact that every frustrated expectation, for example, an expectation due simply to *habit*, can give rise to claims. A child who is accustomed to being kissed by his mother when going to bed experiences a resentful claim, when his mother, absorbed by guests, forgets to perform her "duty." Everybody knows that a favor, regularly bestowed, gives rise to claims on the part of the beneficiary, and the "impulsions" of the benefactor, unilateral at first, can in course of time easily take an imperative-attributive form. Unilateral norms, sufficiently integrated by habit in the minds of people belonging to a group, are usually transformed into bilateral ones. This fact explains why, as the example of Petrazycki shows, it is not easy to quote instances of unilateral norms. They always seem bilateral when they are really binding, and in order to find examples of unilateral norms we must turn either to norms which have never been treated as binding, as is the case of the norm which recommends us to offer the other cheek, or to norms which have been binding in the past but nowadays are treated rather as obsolete, as is the norm "Honor thy mother and thy father" in those countries where mutual love and comradeship have replaced a hierarchical structure of the family.

Thus, if the existence of widely experienced claims is decisive for including the given norm in the class of legal norms, among the really binding norms, practically nothing is left to morality. Even the norm recommending love of one's neighbor, always quoted as a typical example of a unilateral norm, can in some cases be bilateral, as, for example, in the case of maternal love. People disapprove of a mother who does not love her child. The child can claim her warm attention, and the mother herself can feel guilty of disappointing these claims, which she considers valid.

Let us sum up our criticism. As a psychologist, Petrazycki in principle treats the difference between imperative and imperative-attributive obligations as based upon a distinction in the corresponding "impulsions." Whenever X deems himself obliged to perform action A, and thinks of A as owed to another person, his obligation is legal, as, for example, when he pays the agreed wages to his servant. Whenever he does not consider his obligation as due to somebody, his obligation is moral, as is usually the case in giving alms. In this form the distinction of legal and moral rules does not seem operational, since we have always to inquire what is the state of mind of the person who makes use of the norm, and it may easily happen that the same norm, recommended by the same person, is moral at one time and legal at another.

It is probably the need to make the distinction more steady and more predictable which leads Petrazycki to introduce the additional condition that the claim be valid and to reject all unreasonable and absurd claims. Even when he does not speak quite explicitly of validity, although he often does, this condition is felt to be latent in his distinction, while it is introduced *expressis verbis* into the definition of law by B. Malinowski, who, as quoted above, speaks of rightful claims.

Taking into account this additional condition, we faced two possibilities of its interpretation, neither of them free from difficulties. If a claim is rightful, or even only seems rightful, with reference to some norms, we are engaged in a regress. If a claim is rightful in virtue of the fact that it is widely shared, only those norms which are obsolete or have never been binding are left to morality, since all norms really accepted in society seem associated with claims.

We should like to conclude these remarks with some historical considerations. The distinction between legal and moral norms, as discussed above, has been usually associated with the name of Petrazycki, who undoubtedly was the first to develop it at length and made out of it the basic difference between morality and law. But germs of this distinction are to be found already among eighteenth-century writers who oppose charity to justice, considering that the first cannot be required from anybody, while the second is subject to claims. This distinction, treated as a distinction *within* the domain of morality, was later discussed in the fifth chapter of J. S. Mill's *Utilitarianism.* In that chapter Mill dwells upon the concept of justice in connection with the principle of utility. When referring to a distinction of duties of perfect and imperfect obligation he writes as follows:

> Duties of perfect obligation are those duties in virtue of which a correlative right resides in some person or persons; duties of imperfect obligation are those moral obligations which do not give birth to any right. . . . I think it will be found that this distinction exactly coincides with that which exists between justice and the other obligations of morality. . . . It seems to me that this feature in the case—a right in some person, correlative to the moral obligation—constitutes the specific difference between justice and generosity or beneficence. Justice implies something which it is not only right to do, and wrong not to do, but which some individual person can claim from us as his moral right.[5]

This distinction, as we mentioned before, and as is obvious from the passage quoted, is for Mill a distinction of two kinds of *moral* rules. But the rules of justice are, according to him, connected with law. The term "just," as he shows, is derived from "iussum," that is, "that which has been ordered," and is in different languages related to law, while conformity to law is the primitive element in the formation of the notion of justice. Thus the characteristic of rules of justice can be considered as a characteristic of rules of law, which makes the analogy with Petrazycki's distinction still more evident. Later in the same chapter Mill tries to explain what is a right. "When we call anything a person's right, we mean that he has a valid claim on society to protect him in the possession of it, either by the force of law or by that of education and opinion." If somebody should ask why society ought to support this claim, Mill confesses to be able to give no other reason than general utility. The claim, as we see, is addressed here, in his opinion, not to an individual but to society.

There is a further analogy between Mill and Petrazycki which deserves attention: both agree in attributing peculiar importance to bilateral rules. Rules of justice form "the most sacred and binding form of all morality," writes Mill in the same chapter, and "Justice is a name of certain classes of moral rules, which concern the essentials of human beings more nearly." Petrazycki makes a comparison of moral rules to champagne, while legal rules are compared to water—to goose wine, as he used to say. They are much more useful in the life of society and endowed with a much greater motivational force. Thus the conversion of moral consciousness into a legal one always constitutes an important step forward.

The difficulties encountered in Petrazycki's characterization of law and morality do not diminish the respect due to all his valuable contributions in these domains. In both of them he combated with great energy and success all possible forms of fiction. This makes him a successor of Bentham, whose tracking of fictions in morality and law only now begins to be sufficiently appreciated.

[1]Reprinted from the *Journal of Philosophy*, 57 (1960), 251-258.

[2]G. Radbruch, *The Legal Philosophies of Lask, Radbruch and Dubin*, trans. by Kurt Wilk (Cambridge, Mass.: Harvard University Press, 1950), p. 81.

[3]G. del Vecchio, "Homo juridicus," *Droit, Morale, Moeurs* (Paris: Ed. Sirey, 1936), pp. 1-20. The quoted passage is on p. 3.

[4]Bronislaw Malinowski, *Crime and Custom in Savage Society* (London: K. Paul, Trench, Trubner & Co., 1932), p. 55.

[5]John Stuart Mill, *Utilitarianism* (New York: E. P. Dutton Everyman's Library, 1912), p. 46.

CHAPTER

8

Social Engineering through Law

JAN GORECKI

> There is a strong association between murder and the death penalty in the popular imagination [according to the Royal Commission on Capital Punishment].[1] The deterrent force of capital punishment operates not only by affecting the conscious thoughts of individuals tempted to commit murder, but also by building up in the community, over a long period of time, a deep feeling of peculiar abhorrence for the crime of murder. . . . This widely diffused effect on the moral consciousness of society . . . must be at least as important as any direct part which the death penalty may play as a deterrent in the calculations of potential murderers.

This account, if used as the reason for introducing or maintaining capital punishment, would be a genuine instance of the attitude which Roscoe Pound, over fifty years ago, called social engineering through law.[2] This attitude treats legal norms as deliberate tools for policies: those who adopt it have definite social change as their goal, and use the norms to bring about the change. This is exactly the approach of lawmakers who, willing to eradicate murder, would introduce (or maintain) the death penalty to deter potential murderers and to educate the general public.

The approach has broader connotations than implied above: it is not limited to legislative activity, but has been adopted frequently by courts in societies where courts, rather than the legislature, make laws (like common law courts in England or praetors in the Roman Republic). It is also being implemented in the judicial process under the separation of legislative and judicial powers; when constructing norms in force, the courts frequently define terms, make distinctions, and fill gaps with a clear-cut social goal in mind—thus making pseudosyllogistic judicial decisions dependent upon policy considerations.

Leon Petrazycki was probably the most explicit proponent of this approach. He developed a consistent theory of social engineering through law—or of "legal policy," as he called it—in the final decade of the past century. Having done this in Europe, in particular in response to preparatory works on the German civil code, he referred the theory to legislative activity and not to judicial lawmaking; however, his basic notions are relevant to either, and to construction as well.[3] While developing the theory, he faced two basic problems familiar to all those concerned with policy-making: which goals are worth achieving and how can the means to achieve them be discovered.

The Goals

(1) The immediate goals of specific norms may, of course, be innumerable. For example, a norm punishing murder may be purposefully enacted to deter, norms of agency, to expand the scope of business operations, and norms directing traffic along a specific side of the road, to avoid collisions. What Petrazycki does, however, is to introduce an ultimate and universal goal, one which is to be pursued by all lawmakers. The goal is simple: it is the state of universal and active benevolence of men; or, to use Petrazycki's original expression, of "active and rational love." Norms of law should be designed so as to best socialize men toward its achievement.

This apparently sounds like some of the absolutes pronounced by the natural law school. Indeed, Petrazycki praises the school for its idealism, distinguishing it from the positivist legal philosophy prevailing in his day (and later). However, he does not accept the natural law doctrine. The doctrine may be based in particular on any one of the three following assumptions. First, on accepting any religious commandments. Second, on admitting that certain legal norms are in accord with the "nature of things," in particular with "human nature," that is, with universal, biological, or psychological regularities, expressible in terms of scientific knowledge. Third, on assuming that there are some basic norms omnitemporally institutionalized, that is, internalized by all or nearly all men, at any time and in any place.[4]

Petrazycki does not concur with any of the three assumptions. His is not a creed-oriented theory. Neither does he confuse universal statements of scientific knowledge with norms; and he knows the logical nonderivability of the latter from the former. Finally, he does not admit that any norms are institutionalized without any spatiotemporal limitations—a hypothesis too easy to refute on historical or anthropological grounds. Nevertheless, rejecting belief in natural law does not necessarily imply an amoral attitude, as adopted by legal positivists. The positivists limit their interest to the law which is actually in force. They consider its systematic analysis to be the legal profession's only job, and its purely technical amelioration—improving its internal logic and consistency—as the job for lawmakers. According to the "narrowly conceived relativism" of this doctrine, "there cannot exist any criterion out or above the norm of positive law which might be used to evaluate that norm."[5]

Thus, legal positivists avoid the errors of the natural law doctrine: its confusion of what is and what ought to be, and its admission of universally internalized norms. However, with its errors they also reject its idealism and ethical vigor, its basic tendency to make laws (and men) morally better. This explains recurring reactions against positivism, and returns to the notion of the law of nature in this or another form. One conspicuous return—or, strictly speaking, an attempted compromise between the natural law doctrine and positivism—was Stammler's idea of a "natural law with changing contents," which became influential in Europe, and, more recently, in America.[6] However, despite its appeal, this unclear idea could hardly be accepted. Understood literally, it contradicts itself by implying unchanging norms which do change anyway. According to some of its proponents, it denotes just the norms internalized by the majority of a given ethnic group or culture; but why then call them "natural law," and thus misleadingly imply their universal character? In another interpretation, belief that there is natural law with changing contents assumes a somewhat mysterious constant "core" within the otherwise changing provisions; the metaphorical assumption is, however, not precise enough to ever be tested.

Petrazycki accepts the idealism of the natural law school, not its errors. He does not deny that values and norms are man-made, which, however, does not imply that all of them are equally good, or that lawmakers are to be freed from accepting only worthy ones as the basis for legislation.

The benevolence of men is a man-made value. It is, according to Petrazycki's moral code, uppermost: "an axiom of practical reason."[7] Consequently, "it does not require any proof, and could not possibly be proved" by reduction to any other higher level value. "In particular, it would be unsound to attempt to prove its validity by showing its beneficial impact on the welfare of men,"[8] their happiness or pleasures.

Thus, Petrazycki does not join utilitarians, eudaemonists, or hedonists. He is, like utilitarians, a teleologian: norms of law should not be simply right, but should be aimed at a good state of affairs. Since the state consists in human excellence, Petrazycki's is a perfectionist teleology.

Is achievement of the ideal possible? Petrazycki claims that it is, and refers to history for evidence. He finds moral progress in the course of the development of past and present cultures—the Greek, the Roman, and the European since the Middle Ages.[9] The progress consists in better socialization of men, that is, in refinement of the human ethos which brings men closer to the ideal. Petrazycki's sociology explains the progress: it is an outcome of transmitting ethical values in the process of interaction, and of those values which are conducive to the good of the group eventually "winning the referendum."[10] Petrazycki does not consider the process as an outcome of universal laws of social development. Avoiding the historicist error (denounced by Popper a half-century later), he speaks about "developmental tendencies" only. The tendencies do not bring rectilinear evolution; counteracting factors may impede the trend or even reverse it completely, like in the final period of the ancient world. However the tendencies can, and should, be reinforced by purposeful action; that is, by rational social policy toward the ideal. Legal norms are to be used as powerful tools for this policy.[11]

(2) Petrazycki does not claim that the achievement of the ideal of benevolence of men (or of universal love) should become the lawmakers' exclusive goal. It is only the ultimate goal; and there are many other more direct goals which may and should be pursued at various stages of social development. Crime prevention, the enhancement of human dignity, providing incentives for industriousness, economic growth, and the refinement of distribution are among the many goals which Petrazycki recommended to the European lawmakers of his time. All of them may be highly valued in themselves; however, Petrazycki sees their intrinsic value as being "subservient to the universal ideal."[12] Thus, for instance, lawmakers "should always take into account whether the expected economic outcome—related to the production or the distribution of goods—fits the universal, noneconomic ideal";[13] and the same holds true with respect to all other immediate legislative goals.

The Means

How can the lawmakers' goals—the ultimate ideal and the more immediate objectives—be achieved? To rejoin, Petrazycki asks, first, a broader question: how, in general, can legal norms be made into conscious tools for the achievement of goals? Only then does the more specific issue follow: how can legal norms be used to achieve his cherished goal? Thus, his answer to the latter question provides an outline of the social engineering through law method as applied to attain one particular aim, while the answer to the former illuminates the method in general, applicable for attaining any objective.

(1) Let us begin with the first question. Lawmakers are to accumulate, in advance, knowledge of the impact of potential legal norms on human behavior, and to implement only those which will bring about the intended behavior. This entails the "scientifically grounded predictions of effects to be expected in case of the enactment of given legal norms, and making norms which . . . would bring about the intended effects. Consequently, the scientific policy of law should be based upon discovery of . . . the causal influence of law in general, and of its various kinds and elements in particular."[14] This is, of course, a purely technical device, like those applied by engineers or doctors who utilize physics, chemistry, or physiology to build bridges or to treat disease. However, the basic sciences are being replaced here by knowledge of "the causal influence of law." Thus, this knowledge becomes a prerequisite for social engineering.

How can this knowledge be acquired? Since norms of law affect minds and, consequently, the social and economic activities of men, the knowledge is to be founded on psychology, sociology, and economics.[15] Its psychological and economic foundations are of particular import. Legal norms are among the motives of human behavior, and among the educative forces as well: thus, specific knowledge of the motivation and education through law is to be based upon "general psychological knowledge of factors and processes motivating human behavior and bringing about the development of the human character."[16] Moreover, since norms of law, in particular of private law, organize the production and the distribution of goods,[17] whatever economic theory may say on the economic effects of potential legal provisions is an important source of knowledge for the social engineer.[18]

On the whole, much knowledge, in particular that based on psychology and economics, is at hand. Thus, the social engineer can deduce from it and in this way anticipate the effects of many norms which may be enacted. In addition, even commonsense knowledge, however imprecise, often constitutes a valid basis for deduction. For instance, it is generally known that "there are many who are inclined to enrich themselves at the expense of others, in particular if law provides an opportunity."[19] This is, of course, "a very imprecise premise (in terms of measuring the intensity of the inclination, and its change under the impact of factors other than the law.)"[20] Nevertheless, assuming that unfair enrichment is to be avoided, the vague premise can be utilized for very definite criticism of a given legal system and can "provide many useful recommendations for its change."[21] Another obvious statement, that "there are over-trustful, gullible, and inexperienced people who can easily become victims of the egoism of others, or even of their own carelessness or inability to express their thoughts clearly,"[22] is equally imprecise: "it is impossible to determine accurately the proportion of those gullible—or to measure the degree of their gullibility."[23] Nevertheless, if protecting the weak is an accepted legislative goal, the statement may become a viable premise for criticizing and improving many norms of various legal systems—for example, norms regarding the validity of some contracts, the form of contracts, the power of proxy, warranty,[24] and so forth.

With respect to many legislative problems, however, premises provided by the existing scientific or commonsense knowledge will be inconclusive; consequently, "pros and cons will seem equally weighty or, at least, neither of the opposing arguments will definitely prevail."[25] Then the premises will have to be scrupulously tested, which assumes prior "development of the proper methodology . . . the science of experiential testing . . . for the use of legal policy."[26] When projecting the methodology Petrazycki suggests, in particular, one device: utilizing the effects of respective norms of various legal systems to corroborate or refute the general premises of scientific (or commonsense) knowledge. This notion—assuming deductive testing of theories, and thus anticipating future developments in the theory of science[27]—implies a new usage of comparative law (and legal history).

The contribution of legal comparison to the lawmaking process consisted, in Petrazycki's days (and frequently today), in the mere listing of foreign norms: a great many of them "are being set together . . . without considering how they work."[28] The lists, however, "had they been made in even more detail and covered all the states on earth . . . do not prove anything . . . unless it is discovered whether the norms listed had appeared effective or ineffective in action, in what way, and why."[29] Thus, this discovery should become the main concern for policy-oriented comparative lawyers.

The discovery may bring varying conclusions. For instance, a lawmaker aiming at a goal Y may, deducing from his knowledge, conclude that only norm X results in Y, and non-X results in non-Y. If a number of foreign legal systems contain (purposefully or incidentally) the norm

X, and if indeed under all these systems Y follows, the lawmaker's knowledge is corroborated; if Y does not follow, his knowledge is refuted. If, on the other hand, a number of foreign systems do not contain the norm X, the appearance of Y refutes the knowledge, while its absence corroborates it.[30]

Petrazycki was aware of the difficulties involved in this sort of experiential testing, in particular of the multifactorial character of social phenomena; because of this, the appearance of Y may actually be an outcome of unknown conditions other than the norm X, and the nonappearance of Y may be a result of conditions other than the absence of X. He consequently suggests (however, in general terms only) developing a statistical "methodology for the correct evaluation of factual data";[31] this would enable us "to determine whether a given phenomenon, pathological or useful, is, indeed, an outcome of a given legal norm," and not of other factors.[32] He anticipates eventual international cooperation of "thousands of scholars, helping each other, and providing each other with mutual criticism,"[33] to collect "quantitative . . . data on the factual . . . working of contemporary legal norms in force"[34] —a vision of legal comparison hardly anticipated by comparative lawyers not only in the 1890s when these words were written, but even today.

(2) All these general considerations hold with respect to the second of the above questions: how to achieve Petrazycki's particular goal—the ethical education of men. Here, however, since the question is narrower the answer becomes more specific. It rests on one basic assumption: that legal norms do not only directly motivate human behavior but, in the long run, also influence attitudes. "Their impact consists, first, in stimulating or repressing incentives for various acts . . . and, moreover, in enhancing and developing some inclinations and traits of the human character, as well as weakening and eradicating others—briefly, in educating society."[35]

The education consists in the emergence and strengthening of legal impulsions. They emerge and are reinforced in the course of the persistent and uniform application of official law. This is due to acquisition of habit,[36] social imitation,[37] the persuasive force of official law if it "is being held in esteem by the society,"[38] and, especially, in the association of images of punishments or rewards with prohibited or demanded acts.[39] In particular, as an effect of long-lasting association of punishment with prohibited behavior, "the behavior becomes, in the eyes of the nation, abominable, horrible, disgraceful . . . and its opposite is considered fine, praiseworthy, and respectable."[40]

However, the operation of official law does not only bring about and reinforce legal impulsions, but also as it continues, the quality of the impulsions changes from positive to intuitive: they are eventually experienced as just per se, without reference to any normative facts:[41]

> Originally, the legal experiences aroused by the normative facts depend upon images of these facts. Then, especially if they recur frequently and vividly, they become autonomous—independent of the normative facts and their images; thus they change into intuitive legal experiences. The process results from the emergence of lasting associations between images . . . [of behavior prescribed or prohibited], and imperative-attributive impulsions.
>
> The process is, among others, responsible for the peculiar . . . and one-sided development of the intuitive-legal attitudes of those who professionally and permanently deal with various branches of positive law; e.g., legal scholars, judges, attorneys. . . . The positive law which they continuously study, teach, or apply (which they, then, experience frequently . . . and which imprints pertinent dispositions in their minds), becomes to a large extent their intuitive law, and eliminates various elements of the intuitive law previously internalized. Thus, their intuitive legal attitudes differ considerably from those of nonspecialists (which sometimes results in the absence of mutual understanding, controversies, etc.). In the same manner, although weaker and less visibly, does the positive law influence the intuitive-legal attitudes of all other members of the society.[42]

These propositions not only present the impact of official law on attitudes, but also imply an explanation of the impact. There are elements of classical conditioning, instrumental learning, habit acquisition, and imitative learning theories among the above explanatory assumptions. Also present is the declaratory force of law hypothesis, which assumes that the official law's impact is a result of its prestige (or due to the belief that the law reflects prevailing societal views).[43] Of course, other hypotheses might be added to the list, like the assumptions of the cognitive balance theories: those who, due to the impending punishments or rewards of official law, act contrarily to their views, go through the stress of inconsistency—changing their views is one way of "reducing the dissonance."

Whatever its explanation, the hypothesis that official law has an impact on attitudes is fundamental for Petrazycki's social engineering. The impact varies in direction: Official law can not only moralize but can also demoralize society.[44] Its demoralizing effect may be an outcome of the lawmakers' intrinsic immorality. Frequently, however, it emerges as an unintended consequence, due to flaws in the lawmakers' knowledge of the "causal influence of the law." For instance, many draftsmen of statutes, in particular criminal ones,[45] accumulate incentives to bring about the intended behavior and disregard the fact that "one incentive may annihilate the other,"[46] even if each of them, separately, could have been efficient. (This is reminiscent of a familiar error: "A child is interested in learning because of his wish to know, or because he enjoys purposeful work. It is the ill-advised mother who promises him money for every successful lesson. In effect, the wish to be rewarded may diminish or remove the previous motives."[47]) Other demoralizing side effects may result from excessive inculcation, transforming a useful attitude into a shortcoming, for example, thrift into stinginess, or patriotism into chauvinism.[48] Furthermore, lawmakers often disregard the difference between the individual and the social influence of legal norms: "If a norm affects . . . the society at large, the outcome may differ from the impact the norm would have had on isolated individuals. This is due to the multitude of those affected who mutually exchange opinions and feelings."[49] In the process of interaction, the effects of an incentive provided by a legal norm "may become either excessively strong or, on the contrary, decline because of widespread resistance,"[50] which would not have been the case had the norm been affecting only isolated men.

The impact of official law on attitudes varies not only in direction, but also in strength. Its strength depends, to a large extent, upon its congruity with actual social needs and with tendencies of social development. Thus, a backward official law will hinder intuitive law less than a progressive official law will further its development. Sometimes, progressive official law influences the intuitive rapidly and radically:

> It occasionally produces profound "revolutions" in the intuitive law of society. For instance, the abolition of serfdom in Russia,[51] a great legal reform implemented under the impact of intuitive law of those educated and progressive . . . did undoubtedly exceed the development of intuitive law by the majority. The intuitive law of the majority of landlords and the vast majority of peasants had been, until . . . the abolition, a law of lord-slave relationship. The landlords claimed rights to their villains, and the latter assumed respective obligations—not only because of the legal norms in force, but also independently of the norms, according to their conscience, to their intuitive-legal convictions. Many of them had not even imagined any possibility . . . of another legal system. . . . That was exactly where the legislative change produced a speedy and radical upheaval. Some peasants, mainly the older ones, maintained until the end of their lives the old psyche of villains, and did not recognize the reform. They used to assure their landlords that they thought of faithful service as a sacred duty; and they considered proposals of utilizing freedom, or

> being paid for service, as offensive. . . . On the other hand, the huge majority of peasants, in particular the younger and more sensitive ones, quickly overcame their servile intuitive-legal attitudes. . . . Consequently, due to the intuitive-legal upheaval in society, if not for other reasons, another reform, bringing back the old conditions, became unimaginable one year after the abolition, or even earlier. Analogous intuitive-legal upheavals . . . have occurred in the history of various nations. . . . They resulted from great progressive reforms in official law.[52]

Indeed, instances of intuitively legal "revolutions" brought about by change in the official law apparently can be provided by the history of all modern nations. In America, the abolition of slavery and of school segregation, and various norms of the civil rights acts emerge as the closest parallels to the above experience; and many more can be added to the roll—from the Bill of Rights, through the labor law developments on working hours and collective bargaining, to the recent legislative and judicial trends against sex discrimination.

Thus, to summarize, official law can educate society. According to Petrazycki, the education should be consistently aimed at optimal socialization, which would eventually bring about the ideal of general benevolence. The process is to be based upon knowledge of the "causal influence of law," which is to come from psychology, sociology, and economics. The better the knowledge, the more efficient the process, and the easier the elimination of unintended side effects. These general notions can and, according to Petrazycki, should be applied to law-making in any field: civil, constitutional, procedural, and so on.[53] Let us now consider their application to one specific field: criminal law.

Criminal Law as a Tool of Social Engineering

Criminal law should, according to Petrazycki, be used as a conscious tool to achieve two goals. The most obvious goal is to prevent crime; the ultimate and much more important goal is to educate society. Both are interrelated, of course. Petrazycki concentrates on the latter.

The various assumptions which he used to explain the educative force of law have been mentioned above; all of them hold with respect to criminal law. He considers one of them—the associationist—to be particularly important. Norms of criminal law are predominantly inculcated by the association of punishment with prohibited behavior; they thus intensify the "abhorrence of murder, assault, infringement of dignity, robbery, theft, etc." Moreover, and most significantly, as an effect of the "association of the opposite images" they "speed up, support, and strengthen the development of love and respect for one's fellow man" (which, in feedback, "prevents a multitude of pathological facts, both known and unknown to the criminal code").[54]

Accepting associationism as the main explanatory device has one important practical implication: punishment should not only be "unconditionally linked with crime by the law," but should also "follow the crime, in fact, as persistently and inevitably as possible."[55] This requires not only high efficiency in apprehending offenders but also in court fact-finding procedure. This also means a rejection of all those trends and innovations in penology or procedure which, like probation, tend to abolish the categorical, unconditional character of criminal norms, and to "transform them into tentative prescriptions of expediency, to be applied or not according to the specific aims and circumstances of a case."[56]

The transformation, as well as the general laxity in the administration of criminal justice, "would undoubtedly result in such a breakdown of ethical standards in society and a spread of crimes that even the introduction of very severe punishments could not control them."[57] Probation is just one instance. Many other devices (contemporary or implemented after 1896, when these words were written) could be added to the list; for example, all other kinds of suspended sentences, pre-trial bargaining routines, executive clemency if widely applied—whatever the advantages of any of them may be.

The need for making punishment inevitable is particularly acute at lower levels of social development. As indicated above, the lower the level, the more psychological pressure is necessary. To motivate a primitive tribe efficiently, "the possibility of any argument or hope for justification [of prohibited behavior] has to be removed; the law must be as blind and unswerving as the laws of nature."[58] And, indeed, this is how many primitive laws are. Their "blind and unswerving" response is not a result of the lawmakers' rationality. Rather, it is an outcome of the unconscious, "brilliant" adjustment of (intuitive and, eventually, positive) law to the level of social development of the group—the adjustment produced by the process (presented by Lande) of "impulsive induction."

This need for the inevitability of punishment also explains why:

> there work, under primitive laws, some apparently odd and irrational ways of detecting crime and of unmasking the criminal during the trial. In primitive societies, a potential offender usually knows in advance, and takes into account, that if his offence is not detected by men in the usual way, various gods will take care of it; priests with their auguries and other magic means, or forces of nature—e.g., some animals or plants will

denounce the offender, or a deity will demask him on trial if he fails to admit his guilt (trial by ordeal, etc.).[59]

The same need explains the criminal liability of the insane, of children, and even of animals. Due to primitive man's mentality, one cannot expect him to make clear distinctions about responsibility:

> Once he learns that sometimes those who commit prohibited acts are not being punished (due to insanity, etc.), the force of universal and invariable associations will be undermined . . . e.g., of the association of killing a man with the following death of the killer. He is unable to understand . . . why some categories of killing go unpunished, nor does he realize that other categories unceasingly bring punishment nonetheless; he simply concludes that sometimes the killer may avoid punishment. . . . The modern theory of responsibility is very subtle and abstract, and its application requires a highly developed mental life, enabling men to distinguish among proper categories of facts; consequently, its acceptance in a primitive nation would undermine the necessary associations. . . . From this viewpoint, primitive law, associating punishment with some acts without any exception . . . appears in a new perspective. . . . it is not unwise, but adapted to the . . . level of primitive man's ethos and mind. . . . This brings a new, educational justification for the suffering of all the numerous victims of the primitive doctrine of responsibility.
>
> However, in the course of the development of the human intellect, this . . . justification for the brutality of law gradually . . . disappears. . . . Today there is no need for punishment following the harmful behavior of animals or insane men, because we are able to distinguish clearly varying categories of facts and the strength of those associations which are, indeed, necessary will not decline if an animal, a child, or an insane person goes unpunished. . . . On the contrary, application of the primitive theory of responsibility in a more "mature" nation would not only bring unnecessary victims and pain; but due to the acceptance of proper distinctions in other fields—like morality and religion—it would certainly weaken this specific association of notions which is necessary today . . . mislead men, and undermine their ethics.[60]

Petrazycki has extended this associationist and evolutionary approach to the problem of the severity and measure of punishment. To start with its measure—the primitive mind requires unchanging associations, not only of punishment but, furthermore, of inflexible punishment with prohibited behavior. This is one reason why primitive laws are not prone to adjust the measure to the specific circumstances of individual cases, in particular to the amount of guilt—an issue too sophisticated for primitive men. Thus, "instead of numerous subtle distinctions and considerations, there are general categories [of acts] followed by invariable and clear-cut sanctions."[61] There is also another historic reason for this rigidity: the unifying tendency,[62] which is stronger on the lower levels of social development. All this changes during the process of cultural growth. In particular, the amount of guilt can, and should, be taken into account for reasons similar to those which speak against the punishment of children or of the insane. Consequently, modern criminal lawmakers "usually confine themselves to scoring the minimum and maximum penalties, while determination of specific punishment, within these limits is left to the conscience of judges, i.e., to their intuitive law."[63]

Let me turn to the severity of punishment, which is a traditional legislative dilemma. The optimal degree of severity again depends on the level of social development of the group; or, more precisely, on the level of development of the legal culture, that is, of intuitive law and the degree of its inculcation. Consequently, primitive societies "need brutal means."[64] On the other hand, in better developed societies brutal means are not only unnecessary but harmful. They intimidate men who are, anyway, influenced properly by higher motives, like the feeling of duty. The intimidation limits the impact of the higher motives (as mentioned above, Petrazycki claims that accumulating incentives for intended behavior does not necessarily work as reinforcement: sometimes one incentive annihilates the other); and higher motives, in particular "the feeling of duty, bring better performance than fear."[65] Moreover, excessive punishments often go against the intuitive law of the social group. "If the society considers a penalty as unjustly harsh, its application . . . brings sympathy and friendliness for the offender." These feelings may easily become, due to an association of images, "extended to the prohibited acts themselves; which undermines disgust for crime and, sometimes, even results in glorifying the criminal and in favoring harmful behavior."[66]

That is why the severity of penalties tends to decline in the course of social development (within a broader tendency to diminish motivational pressure).[67] One of Petrazycki's examples deals with breach of contract: "On the lower levels of culture, various threats were being used to ensure scrupulous compliance with the law of contracts, e.g., cutting up the delinquent debtor into pieces by his creditors (the Twelve Tables), selling him into serfdom, public whipping until the debt was paid, doubling the debt in case of delay, etc. The history of the law of contracts displays a decline of pressure; today, there remains only the duty to indemnify for the actually inflicted loss [which is not considered a criminal sanction any more]."[68]

The process is not rectilinear.[69] Numerous counteracting factors, like the instability of a given social system, symptoms of its impending disorganization, deficiencies in the administration of justice itself, in particular in apprehending and convicting criminals, all tend to increase the rigidity of punishments.[70] Despite the setbacks, however, the process goes on. It is being implemented in two ways: first, through legislative change; second, through the abolition of the most severe punishments by the courts. This is due to the impact of intuitive law: "history knows many instances of abolishing various cruel criminal statutes, e.g., those providing for capital punishment or for torture . . . under the influence of the changing, more lenient, and humanitarian intuitive law."[71] Of course, the process is not, on the whole, an outcome of the rational and planned action of lawmakers or judges: again, it results rather from the unconscious adjustment of law to the actual level of social development.

To change the process into conscious, rational activity is exactly the role of social engineering. Petrazycki indicates how the change is to be implemented: his associationist and evolutionary assumptions, if true, provide a sound basis for rational punitive policies. They imply the need for inevitability of punishment. They make it possible to settle the problem of mandatory versus flexible penalties and to predetermine optimal severity. They also provide a key to the more specific controversial question which opened this chapter—whether or not capital punishment is to be applied and, if so, should it be mandatory or optional, exceptional or widely applied for a variety of crimes. Petrazycki considers the death penalty to be a cruel means—but being, from the viewpoint of his social ideal, harmful on the highest levels of cultural development it may be beneficial on the lower. Consequently, the answers will differ from the England of the Tudors to the England of today; and, today, it may not be the same for London or New York, or Kampala.

Conclusion

What is the value of the social engineering through law scheme just outlined? The ultimate goal of human benevolence is its crucial element. Thus I will try to appraise the goal first. This will be followed by a comment on the goals-means paradigm and, finally, by a brief general appraisal.

The state of benevolence of men is considered by Petrazycki as the only primary moral good for social policy-makers, especially lawmakers. The good is universal: it is to be pursued by all of them. *All* other goods are secondary: their implementation should never conflict with the achievement of the primary good. Moreover, they are subject to spatiotemporal limitations: whether or not they should be pursued in a society depends upon its level of development. Thus, secondary and limited status is being granted such goods as freedom, equality, fairness, self-respect, opportunity, and happiness.

The ideal of benevolence has long been with us, from the Stoics and the beginning of Christianity through the French Revolution with its explicit stress on fraternity of men. But, whatever its value, it is impossible for any moral system underlying social policies to limit the list of primary goods to the dominance of love. More precisely: the list cannot be limited to any one item. True, the limitation might be imagined in a tribal, authoritarian group; for example, the struggle for survival among foes may conceivably be considered by all tribesmen as the exclusive ultimate value. However, moral monism would never be accepted in a more complex society, in particular in any open society of today: freedom, equality, fairness, self-respect, the sanctity of life, and more are too widely conceived as primary moral values. Consequently, accepting the plurality of primary goods is the only option open for lawmakers. Of course, benevolence may, and should, be one of them, to which I will return soon.

This defense of pluralism may be challenged. The benevolence of men may be considered as a primary moral good to which the other important goods could be reduced: its achievement would bring their achievement as well. This reasoning is, however, unfounded. True, there is much coincidence of practical consequences; however, the consequences are not the same. For example, benevolent feelings may prevail between slaveowners and slaves, and the abolition of slavery may replace them with hatred: the implementation of equality and freedom for all does not necessarily coincide with love of one's fellow men. Thus, no monistic moral system—perfectionist, utilitarian, or other—"can account for some of our strongest moral convictions."[72]

Accepting pluralism has important implications for Petrazycki's goals-means paradigm. Of course, means used by policy-makers—legal norms or other means—are to be evaluated in terms of their efficiency. But efficiency in reaching one ultimate good should not be accepted as the exclusive criterion. If the preservation of slavery would constitute the best means for promoting benevolence, the means would have to be questioned in the light of other primary values. Consequently, Petrazycki's notion of legal norms as means for social engineering may only be accepted with reservation. The notion brings a suitable device for goal-achievement, provided that all relevant primary goods are being taken into account. (This implies the necessity of balancing whenever norms oriented toward various primary goods compete with one another—a difficult venture, involving broad use of the lawmakers' intuition.)

This criticism is not intended to question the greatness of Petrazycki's social engineering scheme. Never has the ideal of moral education through law been expressed more forcefully and consistently. The ideal, which gave rise to all components of Petrazycki's system, deserves approval. The benevolence of men—under whichever name: love, fraternity, solidarity, humaneness—should be accepted as a primary moral good, and its implementation ought to be pursued by lawmakers. When speaking of lawmakers, I mean here, after Petrazycki, all of them irrespective of time and place: the ideal is to be considered universal, and, in this meaning, it is a moral absolute. In another sense, however, it is relative: its introduction was Petrazycki's personal choice, and its acceptance is a personal choice of anybody else (this writer included).

The ideal must, however, be accepted with qualification. Its approval requires taking into account and mutually balancing other ultimate goods. Only when reduced to suitable proportions does it become feasible. To "make men good" is, as Mr. Justice Brandeis rightly indicated in a dictum opening this book, "no small part of the law's function," and not all of it.

[1]*Report of the Royal Commission on Capital Punishment*, London, 1953, Paragraph 59 (p. 20).

[2]Roscoe Pound, *Introduction to the Philosophy of Law* (New Haven, Conn.: Yale University Press, 1922), p. 99.

[3]Petrazycki opposed the idea of judicial social engineering and favored strict, deductive, quasi-mathematical construction of statutes (see on this Peczenik in this volume). However, the construction is always to some extent voluntary (due, among other things, to the ambiguity of terms of which legal norms are made). Thus, there is no possibility of absolute elimination of one type of construction—voluntary or deductive—at the expense of the other; it is only the problem of degree of voluntary versus deductive considerations. Petrazycki and Peczenik are for as strong a stress on the latter as possible, and rightly so. To the extent, however, to which voluntary considerations are unavoidable, they should be rational rather than intuitive—oriented toward achievement of conscious and clearly defined social goals—and this is where social engineering may legitimately enter the judicial process.

[4]The list of assumptions is not complete. For instance, some legal philosophers—from Hobbes to Rousseau to the most conspicuous, recent attempt of John Rawls (*A Theory of Justice* [Cambridge: Harvard University Press, 1971])—base their naturalistic approach

on contractarian tradition; but the notion of social contract has been explicitly rejected by Petrazycki as ficticious and lacking precision. Others, like H. L. A. Hart (*The Concept of Law* [Oxford: Oxford University Press, 1961], pp. 187-195), denote as natural law the few norms the acceptance of which is a necessary condition for the survival of man in *any* society, like norms restricting violence or protecting limited resources.

[5]Jerzy Lande, *Studia z filozofii prawa* (Studies on Philosophy of Law) (Warszawa: P.W.N., 1959), p. 567.

[6]Compare, for example, Philip Selznick, "Sociology and Natural Law," *Natural Law Forum*, 6 (1961), 103-104.

[7]Petrazycki, *Wstep do nauki polityki prawa* (Introduction to the Science of Legal Policy), Polish trans. by Wiktor Leśniewski of the 1896-97 Russian text (Warszawa: P.W.N., 1968), p. 25.

[8]*Ibid.*

[9]Petrazycki, *Wstep do nauki polityki prawa*, p. 26. See also Lande, in this volume.

[10]See Lande in this volume.

[11]My interpretation of Petrazycki differs here from Lande's. According to Lande, the existence of the evolutionary tendencies toward Petrazycki's ideal gives an objective reason for accepting the ideal (see above, p. 32). This is, however, a fallacious point. The existence of tendencies leading society toward some effect does not necessarily imply that the effect is, indeed, valuable. High value of the effect may be made, like all values, only by ourselves, and this seems to be Petrazycki's explicit view (see above text, p. 117).

[12]Petrazycki, *Wstep do nauki polityki prawa*, p. 105.

[13]*Ibid.*

[14]Leon Petrazycki, *Vvedeniie v izucheniie prava i nravstvennosti* (Introduction to the Study of Law and Morality) (3rd ed.; St. Petersburg, 1908), pp. 2-3.

[15]*Ibid.*, p. 4; Petrazycki, *Wstep do nauki polityki prawa*, pp. 45, 56-57, 81, 106-107.

[16]Petrazycki, *Vvedeniie v izucheniie prava i nravstvennosti*, p. 4.

[17]See Lande, in this volume.

[18]Petrazycki, *Wstep do nauki polityki prawa*, pp. 89-90, 107-108, and *Lehre vom Einkommen*, vol. 2, pp. 515-560.

[19]Petrazycki, *Wstep do nauki polityki prawa*, p. 60.

[20]*Ibid.*, pp. 60-61.

[21]*Ibid.*

[22]*Ibid.*

[23]*Ibid.*, p. 62.

[24]*Ibid.*, p. 170; Petrazycki, *Lehre vom Einkommen*, vol. 2, pp. 444ff.

[25]Petrazycki, *Wstep do nauki polityki prawa*, p. 64.

[26]*Ibid.*, p. 66.

[27]Compare Karl R. Popper, *The Logic of Scientific Discovery* (New York: Harper and Row, 1968).

[28]Petrazycki, *Wstep do nauki polityki prawa*, p. 129.

[29]*Ibid.*

[30]Compare *ibid.*, pp. 125-127.

[31]*Ibid.*, p. 143.

[32]*Ibid.*, p. 127.

[33]*Ibid.*, p. 128.

[34]*Ibid.*, p. 125.

[35]Petrazycki, *Vvedeniie v izucheniie prava i nravstvennosti*, p. 3.

[36]Petrazycki, *Teoriia*, vol. 2, p. 690, and *Wstep do nauki polityki prawa*, p. 50.

[37]Petrazycki, *Wstep do nauki polityki prawa*, p. 30.

[38]Petrazycki, *Teoriia*, vol. 2, p. 501.

[39]Petrazycki, *Wstep do nauki polityki prawa*, pp. 34-35.

[40]*Ibid.*

[41]On the difference between positive and intuitive law see Peczenik, pp. 89 of this text.

[42]Petrazycki, *Teoriia*, vol. 2, pp. 501-502.

[43]On a more recent discussion of the two alternative meanings of the hypothesis, see Nigel Walker and Michael Argyle, "Does the Law Affect Moral Judgments?," *British Journal of Criminology* (1964), 570-581; Leonard Berkowitz and Nigel Walker, "Laws and Moral Judgments," *Sociometry* (1967), 410-422.

[44]Petrazycki, *Wstep do nauki polityki prawa*, pp. 29-32, and *Teoriia*, vol. 2, p. 690.

[45]See below in text.

[46]Petrazycki, *Wstep do nauki polityki prawa*, p. 47.

[47]*Ibid.*

[48]*Ibid.*, p. 51.

[49]*Ibid.*, p. 46.

[50]*Ibid.*

[51]In 1861 (editor's note).

[52]Petrazycki, *Teoriia*, vol. 2, pp. 503-504.

[53]Their application to civil law has been summarized in English by Hugh W. Babb, "Petrazhitskii: Science of Legal Policy and Theory of Law," *Boston University Law Review*, 17 (1937), 818-825.

[54]Petrazycki, *Wstep do nauki polityki prawa*, p. 37.

[55]*Ibid.*

[56]*Ibid.*

[57]*Ibid.*

[58]*Ibid.*, p. 329.

[59]*Ibid.*

[60]*Ibid.*, pp. 330-334.

[61]*Ibid.*, p. 333.

[62]Petrazycki, *Teoriia*, vol. 2, p. 491; compare also Lande's, Johnson's, and Peczenik's contributions in this volume.

[63]Petrazycki, *Teoriia*, vol. 2, p. 617.

[64]Petrazycki, *Wstep do nauki polityki prawa*, p. 28.

[65]*Ibid.*, pp. 48-49.

[66]*Ibid.*, p. 40.

[67]Compare Lande's contribution in this volume.

[68]Petrazycki, *Teoriia*, vol. 2, p. 524.

[69]Compare Lande's contribution in this volume.

[70]Petrazycki, *Wstep do nauki polityki prawa*, p. 347.

[71]Petrazycki, *Teoriia*, vol. 2, p. 524.

[72]David Lyons, *Forms and Limits of Utilitarianism* (Oxford: Oxford University Press, 1965), p. XI.

Bibliography

Aristotle. *Posterior Analytics*, II, 13, 9785.

Babb, Hugh W. "Petrazhitskii: Science of Legal Policy and Theory of Law," *Boston University Law Review*, 17 (1937), 793-829.

Berkowitz, Leonard, and Nigel Walker. "Laws and Moral Judgments," *Sociometry*, 30 (1967), 410-422.

Blumer, Herbert. "Comment," *Berkeley Journal of Sociology*, 9 (1964), 118-122.

———. *Symbolic Interactionism*. Englewood Cliffs, N.J.: Prentice-Hall, 1969.

Borucka-Arctowa, M. *O spolecznym dzialaniu prawa* (The Social Function of Law). Warszawa: P.W.N., 1967.

Cain, Maureen E. *Society and the Policeman's Role*. London: Routledge and Kegan Paul, Ltd., 1973.

Cooley, Charles Horton. *Human Nature and the Social Order*. New York: Charles Scribner, 1922.

———. "The Roots of Social Knowledge," *American Journal of Sociology*, 32 (1926), 57-79.

del Vecchio, G. "Homo juridicus," *Droit, Morale, Moeurs*. Paris: Ed Sirey, 1936, pp. 1-20.

Denzin, Norman K. "The Logic of Naturalistic Inquiry," *Social Forces*, 50 (1971), 166-182.

———. *The Research Act*. Chicago: Aldine, 1970.

———. "Theory, Methods and the Observational Act," *Sociale Wetenschappen*, 16e, no. 2 (1973), 75-86.

Durkheim, Emile. *The Division of Labor in Society*, George Simpson, trans. New York: MacMillan, 1964.

Glaser, Barney G., and Anselm L. Straus. *The Discovery of Grounded Theory*. Chicago: Aldine, 1967.

Goffman, Erving. *Encounters*. Indianapolis, Ind.: Bobbs-Merrill, 1961.

———. *Interaction Ritual*. Chicago: Aldine, 1967.

———. *Relations in Public*. New York: Basic Books, 1971.

Goode, William J. "The Theoretical Importance of Love," *American Sociological Review*, 24 (1959), 37-48.

Gurvitch, Georges. *Sociology of Law.* New York: Philosophical Library, 1942.

Gurvitch, S. "Une philosophie intuitive du droit," *Archives de Philosophie du Droit et de Sociologie Juridique*, 3-4 (1931), 403.

Hart, H. L. A. *The Concept of Law.* Oxford: Oxford University Press, 1961.

Hoebel, E. Adamson. "Law and Anthropology," *Virginia Law Review*, 32 (1946), 836-854.

Holmes, Oliver Wendell, Jr. "The Path of the Law," *Harvard Law Review*, 10 (1897), 457-478.

Hutcheson, Joseph Chappell, Jr. *Judgement Intuitive.* Chicago, Ill.: The Foundation Press, Inc., 1938.

Johnson, Harry M. "The Generalized Symbolic Media in Parsons' Theory," *Sociology and Social Research*, 57 (1973), 208-221.

Kantorowicz, Herman (Gnaeus Flavius). *Der Kampf um die Rechtswissenschaft.* Heidelberg, 1906.

Kotarbiński, Tadeusz. *Gnosiology: The Scientific Approach to the Theory of Knowledge.* Oxford: Pergamon Press, 1966.

———. "Petrazycki's Concept of Adequate Theorem in the Light of Earlier Related Doctrines," in *Philomathes*, Studies and Essays in the Humanities in Memory of Philip Merlan, R. B. Palmer and R. Hamerton-Kelly, eds. Netherlands: The Hague, 1971, pp. 350-370.

Krajewski, Władysław. "Projekt klasyfikacji praw nauki" (Suggestions for Classification of the Laws of Science), *Zagadnienia naukoznawstwa*, VIII (1972), 3-31.

Lande, Jerzy. *Studia z filozofii prawa* (Studies on Philosophy of Law). Warszawa: P.W.N., 1959.

Lang, W. "Leona Petrazyckiego krytyka prawa w rozumieniu prawniczym" (Leon Petrazycki's Criticism of the Law as Understood by Lawyers), in *Z zagadnien teorii prawa i teorii nauki Leona Petrazyckiego.* Studia opracowane dla upamietnienia stulecia narodzin (Selected Issues in Leon Petrazycki's Theory of Law and Theory of Science). Studies published to commemorate the centennary of his birth. Warszawa: P.W.N., 1969, pp. 63-66.

Langrod, Georges S., and Michalina Vaughan, "The Polish Psychological Theory of Law," in *Polish Law throughout the Ages*, W. J. Wagner, ed. Stanford, Calif.: Hoover Institution Press, 1970, pp. 306-315.

Lazari-Pawłowska, I. "Tworzenie pojec nauk humanistycznych wedlug koncepcji Leona Petrazyckiego" (Formation of Concepts in Humanities According to Leon Petrazycki), in *Fragmenty Filozoficzne*, ser. 2. Warszawa: P.W.N., 1959, pp. 102 ff.

Levi, E. H. *An Introduction to Legal Reasoning.* Chicago: University of Chicago Press, 1963.

Lindesmith, Alfred, and Anselm L. Strauss. *Social Psychology.* 3rd ed. New York: Holt, Rinehart and Winston, 1968.

Malinowski, Bronisław. *Crime and Custom in Savage Society.* London: K. Paul, Trench, Trubner & Co., 1932.

Manis, Jerome G., and Bernard N. Meltzer, eds. *Symbolic Interaction.* 2nd ed. Boston: Allyn and Bacon, 1972.

Mead, George Herbert. *Mind, Self and Society.* Chicago: University of Chicago Press, 1934.

———. *Movements of Thought in the Nineteenth Century.* Chicago: University of Chicago Press, 1936.

———. "The Psychology of Punitive Justice," *American Journal of Sociology,* 23 (1917), 557-602. Reprinted in *Selected Writings: George Herbert Mead,* Andrew J. Reck, ed. Indianapolis, Ind.: Bobbs-Merrill, 1964, pp. 212-247.

Mill, John Stuart. *Utilitarianism.* New York: E. P. Dutton, Everyman's Library, 1912.

Olivecrona, K. "Is a Sociological Explanation of Law Possible?," *Theoria,* XIV/2 (1948), 177-178.

Opałek, K. *Problemy metodologiczne nauki prawa* (Methodological Problems of Legal Science). Warszawa: P.W.N., 1962.

———. "Teoria Petrazyckiego a wspolczesna teoria prawa" (Petrazycki's Theory and Modern Jurisprudence), in *Z zagadnien,* 122ff., 130ff.

———, ed. *Z zagadnien teorii prawa i teorii nauki Leona Petrazyckiego. Studia opracowane dla upamietnienia stulecia narodzin.* Warszawa: P.W.N., 1969.

Parsons, Talcott. "Christianity," in *International Encyclopedia of the Social Sciences,* David L. Sills, ed. New York: Macmillan and the Free Press, 1968, vol. 2, pp. 425-446.

———. "Commentary on Clark," *Sociological Inquiry,* 42 (1972), 299-308.

———. "Culture and Social System Revisited," *Social Science Quarterly,* 53 (1972), 253-266.

———. "Equality and Inequality in Modern Society, or Social Stratification Revisited," *Sociological Inquiry,* 40 (1970), 13-72.

———. *Politics and Social Structure.* New York: The Free Press, 1969.

———. *Societies: Evolutionary and Comparative Perspectives.* Englewood Cliffs, N.J.: Prentice-Hall, 1966.

———. *Sociological Theory and Modern Society.* New York: The Free Press, 1967.

———. "Some Problems of General Theory in Sociology," in *Theoretical Sociology, Perspectives and Developments,* John C. McKinney and Edward A. Tiryakian, eds. New York: Appleton-Century-Crofts, 1970, pp. 27-68.

———. *Structure and Process in Modern Societies.* Glencoe, Ill.: The Free Press, 1960.

———. *The Structure of Social Action: A Study in Social Theory with Special Reference to a Group of Recent European Writers.* New York and London: McGraw-Hill, 1937.

———. *The System of Modern Societies.* Englewood Cliffs, N.J.: Prentice-Hall, 1971.

Peczenik, A. "Analogy from Statutes in Continental Law," *Proceedings of the World Congress for Legal and Social Philosophy* (1971), 3-9.

———. "The Concept of 'Valid Law,'" *Scandinavian Studies in Law,* 16 (1972), 211-251.

———. *Juridikens metodproblem.* Stockholm: Almquist and Wiksell, 1974.

———. *Wartosc naukowa dogmatyki prawa* (The Scientific Value of the Doctrinal Study of Law). Kraków: Zeszyty Naukowe U.J., 1966.

Perelman, Chaim, and L. Olbrechts-Tyteca. *La Nouvelle Rhétorique, Traité de l'Argumentation.* Paris: Presses universitaires de France, 1958.

Petrazycki, Leon. *Bona fides v grazhdanskom prave* (Bona Fides in Civil Law). St. Petersburg: N. I. Martinov, 1897.

———. *Die Lehre vom Einkommen.* Berlin: Verlag von H. W. Müller, 1895. Vol. 2.

———. *Law and Morality: Leon Petrazycki*, Hugh W. Babb, trans. Cambridge: Harvard University Press, 1955.

———. *Nowe podstawy logiki i klasyfikacji umiejetnosci* (New Foundations of Logic and Classification of Sciences). Warszawa: Wyd. im. Petrazyckiego, 1939.

———. *O ideale spolecznym i odrodzeniu prawa naturalnego* (Social Ideal and Revival of Natural Law). Warszawa: L. Idzikowski, 1925.

———. *O motivakh chelovicheskikh postupkov* (On the Motives of Human Behavior). St. Petersburg: E. L. Prokhovshchikov, 1904.

———. *Teoriia prava i gosudarstva v sviazi s teoriei nravstvennosti* (Theory of Law and State in Connection with a Theory of Morality). 2nd ed. St. Petersburg: Ekateringofskoe Pechatnoe Delo, 1909-10.

———. Polish translation: *Teoria prawa i panstwa w zwiazku z teoria moralnosci*, Jerzy Lande and Wiktor Leśniewski, trans. Warszawa: P.W.N., 1959-60.

———. *Universitet i nauka* (The University and Science). St. Petersburg, 1907.

———. *Vvedeniie v izucheniie prava i nravstvennosti* (Introduction to the Study of Law and Morality). 3rd ed. St. Petersburg: J. N. Erlich, 1908.

———. Polish translation: *Wstep do nauki prawa i moralnosci*, Jerzy Lande, trans. Warszawa: P.W.N., 1959.

———. "Vvendeniie v nauku politiki prava" (Introduction to the Science of Legal Policy), *Universitetskaiia Isvestiia*, 8-10 (1896-97), 1-250.

———. Polish translation: *Wstep do nauki polityki prawa*, Wiktor Leśniewski, trans. Warszawa: P.W.N., 1968.

Popper, Karl R. *The Logic of Scientific Discovery.* New York: Harper and Row, 1968.

Pound, Roscoe. *Introduction to the Philosophy of Law.* New Haven, Conn.: Yale University Press, 1922.

Rawls, John. *A Theory of Justice.* Cambridge, Mass.: Harvard University Press, 1971.

Report of the Royal Commission on Capital Punishment. London, 1953.

Ross, A. *On Law and Justice.* Berkeley: University of California Press, 1959.

Schmidt, F. "Construction of Statutes," *Scandinavian Studies in Law*, 1 (1957).

———. "Model, Intention, Fault. Three Canons for Interpretation of Contracts," *Scandinavian Studies in Law*, 4 (1960), 177-207.

Selznick, Philip. "Sociology and Natural Law," *Natural Law Forum*, 6 (1961), 103-104.

Simmel, Georg. *The Sociology of Georg Simmel*, Kurt Wolff, trans. New York: Free Press, 1950.

Smelser, Neil J. *Essays in Sociological Explanation*. Englewood Cliffs, N.J.: Prentice-Hall, 1968.

———. *Social Change in the Industrial Revolution. An Application of Theory to the British Cotton Industry*. Chicago: University of Chicago Press, 1959.

Sorokin, Pitirim A. *Society, Culture and Personality*. Rev. ed. New York: Cooper Square Publishers, 1962.

———. *Sociological Theories of Today*. New York: Harper and Row, 1966.

Stone, Gregory P., and Harvey Farberman, eds. *Social Psychology through Symbolic Interaction*. Waltham, Mass: Ginn-Blaisdell, 1970.

Strauss, Anselm L. *Mirrors and Masks*. San Francisco: Sociology Press, 1969.

Suttles, Gerald D. "Friendship as a Social Institution," in *Social Relationships*, George J. McCall, *et al.*, eds. Chicago: Aldine, 1970, pp. 95-135.

Timasheff, Nicholas S. *An Introduction to the Sociology of Law*. Cambridge, Mass.: Harvard University Press, 1939.

———. "Growth and Scope of Sociology of Law," in *Modern Sociological Theory in Continuity and Change*, Howard Becker and Alvin Boskoff, eds. New York: Holt, Rinehart and Winston, 1959, pp. 424-449.

Turner, Ralph. *Family Interaction*. New York: John Wiley and Sons, 1970.

Viehweg, Theodor. *Topik und Jurisprudenz*. München: Beck, 1953.

Walker, Nigel, and Michael Argyle. "Does the Law Affect Moral Judgments?," *British Journal of Criminology* (1964), 570-581.

Waller, Willard W. *The Old Love and the New: Divorce and Readjustment*. Philadelphia, Pa.: Horace Liveright, Inc., 1930.

Weber, Max. *The Theory of Social and Economic Organization*, A. M. Henderson and Talcott Parsons, trans. New York: Oxford University Press, 1947.

Woleński, J. *Metodologiczne dazenia Petrazyckiego a wspolczesna teoria nauki* (Petrazycki's Methodology and Modern Theory of Science), *Z zagadnien.*

Wróblewski, J. "Jezyk a nauka w teorii Leona Petrazyckiego" (Language and Science in Leon Petrazycki's Theory), *Z zagadnien.*

Zajkowski, J. "Wykladnia ustaw wedlug Petrazyckiego i wedlug jego teorii" (Construction of Statutes According to Petrazycki and His Theory), *Wileński Przeglad Prawniczy* (1936), 11-27.

Contributors

NORMAN K. DENZIN, Professor of Sociology, University of Illinois, Urbana. He is the author or co-author of eight books, which include *The Research Act, Children and Their Caretakers* (editor), and *Social Psychology* (with A. R. Lindesmith and A. L. Strauss).

JAN GORECKI, Professor of Sociology, University of Illinois, Urbana. He has been Associate Professor, University of Cracow Law School; Foreign Universities Exchange Scheme Visitor, University of London; Fellow, Center for Advanced Study in the Behavioral Sciences, Stanford. His English publications include *Divorce in Poland—A Contribution to the Sociology of Law.*

HARRY M. JOHNSON, Professor of Sociology, University of Illinois, Urbana. He has been Visiting Professor at the Salzburg Seminar for American Studies, Columbia University, and University of Munich. His publications include *Sociology: A Systematic Introduction.*

TADEUSZ KOTARBIŃSKI, Professor of Philosophy, University of Warsaw. Dr. *honoris causa*, universities of: Brussels, Lodz, Cracow, Florence, Oxford, Bratislava. He has been President of the Polish Academy of Sciences and of the International Institute of Philosophy. His English publications include *Gnosiology—The Scientific Approach to the Theory of Knowledge*, and *Praxiology—An Introduction to the Sciences of Efficient Action.*

JERZY LANDE (d.1954), Professor and Head of the Chair of Theory of Law, University of Cracow Law School.

MARIA OSSOWSKA (d.1974), Professor of Moral Philosophy, University of Warsaw. She has been Head of the Chair of History of Moral Theory at Warsaw University, and Visiting Professor at the University of Pennsylvania. Her English publications include *Social Determinants of Moral Ideas.*

ALEXANDER PECZENIK, Associate Professor, University of Stockholm Law School. He has been Associate Professor, University of Cracow Law School, and Head of the Chair of Legal Methodology, University of Katowice. His English publications include *Essays in Legal Theory.*

Index